ACPL ITEM P9-ECS-895

DISCARDED

f**P**

Immortal Milk

ADVENTURES IN CHEESE

—

Eric LeMay

Free Press

New York ~ London ~ Toronto ~ Sydney

P

Free Press
A Division of Simon & Schuster, Inc.
1230 Avenue of the Americas
New York, NY 10020

First Free Press hardcover edition June 2010

FREE PRESS and colophon are trademarks of Simon & Schuster, Inc.

For information about special discounts for bulk purchases,
please contact Simon & Schuster Special Sales at 1-866-506-1949
or business@simonandschuster.com.

The Simon & Schuster Speakers Bureau can bring authors to your live event.
For more information or to book an event, contact the Simon & Schuster
Speakers Bureau at 1-866-248-3049 or visit our website at
www.simonspeakers.com.

Designed by Julie Schroeder

Manufactured in the United States of America

10   9   8   7   6   5   4   3   2   1

Library of Congress Cataloging-in-Publication Data
LeMay, Eric Charles.
    Immortal milk : adventures in cheese.
        p. cm.
    I. Title.
    SF271.L46 2010
    641.3'73—dc22
                                        2009036155
ISBN 978-1-4391-5304-8
ISBN 978-1-4391-5908-8 (ebook)

continued on p. 246

Contents

It may be dull, it may be naive, it may
be oversophisticated. Yet it remains cheese,
milk's leap toward immortality.

—Clifton Fadiman

as I was crawling
through the holes in
a swiss cheese
the other
day it occurred to
me to wonder
what a swiss cheese
would think if
a swiss cheese
could think and after
cogitating for some
time I said to myself
if a swiss cheese
could think
it would think that
a swiss cheese
was the most important
thing in the world

—Archy the cockroach,
from Don Marquis's "archygrams"

Immortal Milk

Stilton with Jane Austen

*C*onsider the Stilton.

Its marbled blues entice the eye. Its spiny mold pricks the nose. Its salt stings, its cream soothes, its metal commands the mouth. Stilton isn't cheese. Stilton is a state of being.

I had this realization while watching the BBC's recent adaptation of *Sense and Sensibility*. To celebrate its release, the heroine of my own love story, Chuck, had assembled some English cheeses. We had a stodgy Red Leicester, a tangy Cheshire, a biscuity Lancashire, and a Cheddar so full of sweet grass and rich butter we felt bucolic. But when we tasted the Stilton, our conversation about the cheese, the costumes, the adaptability of the novel in general and Austen in particular stopped. Awe enveloped us. Speech abandoned us. We were Stiltoned.

I don't know how long this state lasted: Stilton lingers on your tongue as though it were whiling away a rainy afternoon in an English manor. But I do know my daze ended when I heard a snicker. I blinked myself back.

"You're grunting," said Chuck.

I listened. I was.

Chuck laughed, and instead of watching, we began musing about why the Stilton was so spellbinding. Did it trigger some English gene that had been latent in us since the Revolutionary War? Did it evoke the tastes we'd imagined when we'd watched those grand dinners in Jane Austen movies? Or did it just taste good, without a why?

Here's my answer: We were enthused. When we were eating the Stilton, when I was swinishly grunting, the Stilton was enthusing us with its creamy, salty, moldy, stenchy self.

"Enthuse?" you might ask, as Chuck did.

That word sounds weird, but then so is the experience I'm describing. "Enthuse" comes from a Greek origin, *entheos*, which means "to be inspired or possessed by god." It shares a root with "theology" and a prefix with "enthrall," "entice," and "enchant." When you're enthused, you're deeply "in" something, though in no ordinary sense. You're caught up, taken over. You're seized by what enthuses you. It may be a god, as in "the spirit is in me." It may be an *Emma*, as in "I'm lost in this book." And it may be a Stilton. Enthused, you sing hosannas and hallelujahs. Enthused, you read until three in the morning and oversleep. Enthused, you grunt.

If "enthused" still sounds weird, then you might compare the enthusiast with the expert. An expert isn't taken over by something, but through knowledge and know-how, masters it. An expert remains unmoved, detached, out ("ex") of a thing's power. "Expert" shares its root with "experience" and "peril," which suggests that an expert not only becomes wise through trying and testing things, but also undergoes trials, takes risks.

An expert heads out and confronts what an enthusiast leaps into and embraces. An expert doesn't grunt.

So, an expert will tell you that Stilton is named after a small village to the north of London where it's illegal to make Stilton. In fact (experts say "in fact" a lot), only seven dairies in England are allowed to make Stilton because the cheese has a special status, a "Protected Designation of Origin," from the European Commission, so that other cheesemakers can't use the name. And an expert will tell you that the name Stilton was first mentioned in 1722 by William Stukeley, who also helped invent archeology and excavate Stonehenge, but it was made famous by Cooper Thornhill, who lived in the village of Stilton and owned the Bell Inn. Thornhill discovered the cheese at a nearby farm. He loved it so much that he began bringing it to Stilton in bulk and selling it to travelers who passed through town on the Great North Road that linked London to northern England. His cheese trade thrived, and word of "Stilton" spread throughout the country until the town and the cheese became synonymous. An expert will also tell you—

"Maybe we should close the computer," suggested Chuck. By "we" she meant me.

Not everyone likes hearing from experts, particularly when expertise gets read aloud from Web sites. Experts, it turns out, aren't quite as likeable as Jane Austen.

Yet, experts can enhance our enthusiasm.

A philosopher I once met suggested that, instead of talking about experts and enthusiasts, I should use the French distinction between *amateur* and *connaisseur*. At the root of *amateur*, he told me, lies the Latin verb *amare*, "to love," while *connaisseur* comes from the verb "to know," and wasn't love what I wanted?

I did, but at that moment I also wanted to know why the French always have a way to say something that, as French speakers will quickly tell you, can't be said in English. *Le mot juste, préciser, je ne sais quoi*. Whenever I'm around French phrase droppers, I feel as though my English comes from a Dumpster.

Much later, and after a long time of figuring that the philosopher must be right, I had an *esprit de l'escalier*. I realized that we want to know what we love. Knowledge and love, as those early translations of the Bible hint ("And Adam knew Eve his wife; and she conceived"), can be very close, and knowing more can lead to loving more. That's probably why we seek out experts. We get enthused by Stilton or Jane Austen and we take an evening course on the Regency novel or read aloud from the Stilton Cheesemakers' Association Web site, because we believe that what experts have to tell us can be a boon. As much as the philosopher was right—as much as I wanted to stress love—I didn't want to divide it from knowledge. I also didn't want to write about "my amorousness for cheese." So, I decided to stick with English, with expertise and enthusiasm, and with a new appreciation for the sparks that fly between the enthusiast's love and the expert's knowledge.

Still, that didn't change the fact that experts can sometimes be bores.

Experts may enhance, may even share our love, but often

enough, through footnote, fact, and figure, they turn what once possessed us into material fit for library shelves or Power-Point. Often, we leave experts less enthused than we arrived.

What, I wondered, would a book about cheese look like if it sprang not from expertise but enthusiasm? Would it be full of exclamations? Would it be void of facts? Would it honor a reader's enthusiasm rather than punish it?

I went looking for one. I found a lot of excellent guide-books: guides to French cheeses, guides to Italian cheeses, guides to the cheeses of the world and the cheeses of Vermont. I found a few books on single cheeses. In an essay called "Cheese," I found G. K. Chesterton's winking promise to publish a five-volume book on *The Neglect of Cheese in European Literature*. I found books by New Yorkers who'd left New York to travel the country in search of the perfect goat cheese or become cheesemakers in Vermont and I greenly wondered why Chuck and I hadn't bought a homestead with sheep. I found a few cool blogs. But what I didn't find was a book that spoke to my experience of eating a Stilton, not even Trevor Hickman's thoroughly researched *The History of Stilton Cheese*. So I resolved to write one.

I turned to Jane Austen for help.

Fortunately, she has a scene in which Stilton figures.

It's in *Emma*, early on, when Emma is trying to make a match between the uppish Mr. Elton and her lowly friend, Harriet. Emma leaves the two alone so love can bloom between them and, when she spies them from a distance, she feels hopeful: "Mr. Elton was speaking with animation,

Harriet listening with a very pleased attention." Her match-making looks as though it's working. Alas, Emma soon learns with "some disappointment" that what animated Mr. Elton and pleased Harriet was, among other things, "the Stilton cheese."

Like Emma, I value love, but unlike her, I think love and cheese go together. This book celebrates that match. Each chapter takes up a question I've had. Why do we relish cheese? What cheese facts does a cheese lover need to know? How is cheese made and who makes it best? What does cheese have to do with being cheesy? Why does cheese comfort us, even when it reeks? And what, when glimpsed as a whole, does the world of cheese look like?

In my search for answers, I've dragged Chuck as near as Formaggio Kitchen in Cambridge, Massachusetts, and as far as the Slow Food International Cheese Festival in Bra, Italy. We've endured surly cheesemongers in Paris and dodged piss-ing goats in Vermont; we've looked down into curd and up at the cosmos; we even climbed a snow-encrusted, lynx-trodden mountain.

By sharing with you the answers we've found on these adventures, we hope to echo Mr. Elton's animation and deepen your love for cheese.

Illegal Cheese

(OR, THE CHEESES WE MET IN FRANCE
FOUND US TOLERABLE)

*S*mugglers shouldn't be users.

I knew this narcotics-trafficking truism from the crime movies I've imbibed over the years, movies in which an imposing drug lord or cartel *jefe* has to clean up after some toady who should have delivered three keys of coke but falls short because, as the squirming toady eventually confesses, "I had to has me a taste!" The cleanup usually involves the toady's skull spattering on a white wall. These scenes always struck me as forced, even for Hollywood. Surely, a real professional would never let his desire so grossly skewer his judgment. Surely, he'd know how it—and he—would end.

Yet, as I walked toward the U.S. Customs and Border Patrol, with a huge scarlet "A" (for "Animal Products") scrawled on my declaration form and six shrink-wrapped bundles of illegal cheese stuffed in my suitcase, I understood the toady. I didn't care about the inspectors glowering at me above their mustaches or the consequences of breaking a federal law. I cared about the cheese. What if they opened it and spoiled it? What if they took it? Would I have time to jam any in my mouth? I had come too far with it, waited too long. I had to has me a taste.

How did this happen? How did I devolve into a lawless, heedless, wholly obsessed cheese smuggler?

The answer is that I was returning from Paris, where Chuck and I had spent a summer roving the city's banks and *îles*, bridges and boulevards.

And Paris, as it's famed to do, alters Americans. You go full of Yankee steam, hell-bent on seeing the Place des Vosges and ascending Sacré-Coeur before you bolt down a croissant while walking to your afternoon at the Louvre. Then, you arrive, and the steam leaks out of you as the Paris light pours in. It hits you when you land, achy from the international flight, your internal clock lagging heavily within you. You drag yourself out of Charles de Gaulle and you blink. It's bright. Bright is everywhere. The sun is high and infectious, and suddenly, instead of collapsing, you feel an intense need to be there already, in the Luxembourg Gardens, under the lime trees, and just what was the name of that café, the one named after the poet, with the striped awning and the *pommes frites?* Later, when you wake at some deep hour of the night, unaware of how long you've slept (for at last you've slept), you wander down the Rue de la Cité, and the Cité bathes you in amber light. The face of Notre Dame pulses in Monet hues. The lamps glisten. And there's the Eiffel Tower, right there, not looking nearly so kitschy as you'd expected, so you wait for its strobe light to come around again, and it does, and you smile.

Chuck and I succumbed to Paris's light as quickly as any Americans. Before we'd left, we'd made lists—lists of paintings to appreciate, churches to admire, day trips to take and galleries to tick off. But the light wouldn't let us. It lured us onto warm benches overlooking the Seine or coaxed us into a second glass of Tavel. So, before long, we did what it wished: We relaxed, we discovered.

And what we discovered, when it demanded we nab yet another snack, was cheese, French cheese, cheese like you've never had cheese if you've had cheese only in America.

You see, in France, cheese isn't caught in the stranglehold of murderous laws. I mean this literally. The Brie or Camembert you buy in America has been murdered.

Let me explain. Cheese, as you know, comes from milk, and milk from cows, goats, sheep, and the odd water buffalo. Now, if this milk isn't extracted by a machine out of the abused udders of animals that are caged in steel stalls, injected with hormones, and fed on bioengineered fodder, if instead this milk comes from Alpine or Saanen goats that have been raised by farmers for generations and herded through the Loire Valley's rich pastures all spring and summer so that the goats can munch on lush grass, clover, wildflowers, and herbs, then this milk will have a flavor unlike any other in the world. It will express the whole of its creation—the land on which it's made, the animals from which it's made, and the people who make it. In its *terroir*, cheese is like wine, as bound to the land as the vines that yield Sancerre or Saumur-Champigny. Think of goats as big, fluffy grapes.

Here's the problem: The delicacy and nuance of flavor that make cheese a supreme expression of place come from microorganisms that live in the milk, and it's these minuscule flavor-makers that the FDA demands farmers kill. You might not be a fan of bacteria. You might consider Louis Pasteur a hero. However, when milk gets pasteurized, the bacteria and enzymes that were in the raw milk die and, with them, much of the milk's flavor.

The FDA would have you fear that raw-milk cheese will cause diseases such as listeriosis or salmonellosis, and if you're pregnant, elderly, or have a weak immune system, this might be true, but in France, where these microorganisms aren't heated out of existence or left to die over a span of sixty days as U.S. law requires, most of the cases of food poisoning that do involve cheese are the result of pasteurized cheeses. Sure, there are bad bacteria, but cheesemakers can avoid them without murdering their milk. They've done so for centuries in the Pyrénées mountains and the hamlets of Provence.

Of course, if you don't care about the rare flavors that milk can create or if you need to ship your milk to a factory, pasteurization is great. By extending milk's shelf life, it allows you to make cheese en masse, like the monstrous Kraft Foods. (Kraft makes that pasteurized, processed, cheese product that bears our name: American cheese.) Pasteurization also makes your milk consistent. As cheesemonger Pierre Androuët explains, "All pasteurized-milk cheeses of whatever sort, mild or strong, have one point in common with respect to their flavor: their blandness."

Androuët is kind. More often than not, when artisan

cheesemakers, mongers, and enthusiasts taste a cheese that's been cleansed of its living, taste-giving microorganisms, they'll say it's "dead."

"This cheese is like—'Fuck off.'"

It's a challenge to describe the flavor of an excellent French cheese. Chuck and I were in our tiny rental in the Marais, hovering over a Langres. This cheese, as it's described in one rather bland guide,

> originates from the high plains of Langres in Champagne. It is shaped like a cylinder and has a deep well on top called a *fontaine*, a kind of basin into which Champagne or *marc* may be poured. This is a pleasant way to eat this cheese, and is characteristic of wine-producing regions.

We didn't have the funds for Champagne, but we had managed to get tipsy on a serviceable *vin de pays*, which is also a pleasant way to eat a Langres.

"It doesn't play well with others," Chuck continued, the thick smack of *pâte* slowing her speech. *Pâte* is the pasty center of the cheese, as opposed to the rind, and as she worked it, she said, "It doesn't respect lesser cheese."

"It's like a road trip through Arizona in an old Buick," I offered.

"It's like Charlus, but early in Proust."

"It has a half-life inside your teeth."

"It has ideas."

"It gradually peels off the skin on the roof of your mouth."

"It attains absolute crustiness and absolute creaminess."

The problem with most descriptions of cheese, the sort you find in guides, is that they're reductive. Officially, the Langres is sticky, wet, shiny, firm, and supple, "melts in the mouth," and has "a complex mixture of aromas." Such descriptions convey, at best, a blueprint of the tasting experience, like a score does a symphony. They're useful, I suppose, in their reliability. Anyone can read that a salt-washed Langres is "salty," then taste its saltiness, but not everyone will taste in it the brilliant and irascible character of Marcel Proust's Palamède de Guermantes, baron de Charlus. Yet these more personal descriptions capture the experience of a Langres. It sparks associative leaps, unforseen flashbacks, inspired flights of poetry and desire. Its riches reveal your own. W. H. Auden once remarked that when you read a book, the book also reads you. The same holds true for cheese: It tastes you.

On the whole, the cheeses we met in Paris found us tolerable. A Signal Savoyard that cracked in our mouth like a mudcake appreciated our humility. It had seen more of the world than we had, and we deferred to it. A Rocamadour saw that, although we were Americans, we could appreciate the fleshier, creamier forms that fill the canvases of Rubens and Fragonard. "It responds like chub," said Chuck, poking at the cheese and her tum. We were plucky enough for a Tomme de Brebis, which tried to toughen us up with sharp punches to the palate. And a floral Pélardon believed that our urban lives hadn't ruined us for country pleasures, that we could still feel idyllic. "This," Chuck declared, "is what a milkmaid's cheeks should taste like."

*   *   *

Why is cheese so delicious?

You'll find a few answers out there, but none of them are entirely satisfying. There's an appeal to history: Since humans first cultivated goats and sheep, about 10,000 years ago (give or take a few millennia), they've made cheese. For evidence, you can cite a Sumerian frieze from around 3,000 B.C.E. that refers to cheese, and cheesemaking appears on a mural in an Egyptian tomb that's roughly the same age. There's also the cyclops in Homer's *Odyssey*. He has a cave full of homemade cheeses and keeps his one eye on the goats and ewes he milks to make them. By the rise of classical Rome, cheesemaking was an art. In his *Natural History*, Pliny the Elder catalogs the variety of cheeses that Romans eat, and in *De Re Rustica*, Columella describes a process of cheesemaking not so different from some used today. Cheese has been around for a long time.

Still, that doesn't explain why it's good. At best, the history of cheese, as well as its presence throughout much of the world, proves it's a survivor. No dodo of food, cheese thrives in cultures and climes as diverse as Canada and India. Cheese can even come back from extinction, as in the case of the wonderful Garrotxa from Spain. Yet cheese has survived in part because it's good; it isn't good because it has survived. To say it another way, cheese isn't delicious just because it's *been* delicious.

And it's not delicious because it's nutritious either. That's another answer you'll find: Cheese has protein, vitamins, calcium, phosphorus, and may even prevent tooth decay. I suppose cheesemakers need to woo the huge demographic of

Americans watching their saturated fat and waistlines, but *ugh*. Who'd want to eat with them? Pleasure doesn't matter when you see food as chemistry, and "deliciousness" doesn't appear under the "Nutritional Facts" on food labels. Let the inch pinchers and heart healthies know: Cheese can't be reduced to a deadening list of dietary facts. It teems with too much life.

This liveliness may be the very reason cheese is delicious. Max McCalman, the *maître fromager* at Artisanal Fromagerie Bistro & Wine Bar in Manhattan, notes the link between cheese and life. Cheese, he says, is "the ancient, venerable method of preserving the precious, sustaining fluid of the mother animal." He's talking about milk, that very first taste which ewes, kids, and calves experience. I'll add us. We're another mothered animal, and milk is our original flavor, the primordial way we're given life. Milk is what we fixate on before we can focus, when we're little more than pudgy mouths at the nipple. Indeed, the psychoanalyst (and Frenchman) Jacques Lacan famously claimed that these milky moments, before we're aware of the world beyond ourselves or even that we have selves distinct and tragically cut off from the warm breast that feeds us, are as close as we'll ever come to paradise. In milk, we taste Eden.

And milk is the essence of cheese. Cheese is milk in its most concentrated form. (You need about ten pounds of cow's milk to make one pound of cheese.) When you ingest cheese, you mainline the uncut elixir of life.

No wonder I'd break laws for it.

*   *   *

Yet, if milk's life-giving flavor is an answer, it's only half an answer. The other half lies in a cheese called Livarot, which we discovered when we chanced on perhaps the finest *fromager* in Paris, Pascal Trotté.

His shop is a modest one on the Rue Saint-Antoine, a few blocks west of the Bastille. Outside, a chalkboard describes the current state of the cheeses, which when we arrived were benefitting from the fresh spring grasses. Inside, it's a gauntlet. Rows of cheese flank you and fill your nose with a rich huff of rind and sweetness, and though there aren't many, each cheese has a place and a placard. The smaller cheeses are piled in pyramids or baskets, and the larger ones subtly glow with more shades of butter and cream than you knew existed. If you linger, you'll see pictures of the caves where the cheeses are aged, for Pascal Trotté is also an *affineur*, which means he's gotten his cheeses from their makers before they're ripe and he's aged them to perfection.

But you probably won't linger. The shop's size, about the width of a grocery aisle, forces you on one of the cheesemongers, who's likely to fix you with that expressionless look Parisians reserve for Americans: "I acknowledge you are human, but that is all I acknowledge."

That, at least, is how we interpreted the stare of the striking corvine man in his late forties who may or may not have been Pascal Trotté.

Chuck is the one of us who has French, so she asked about the cheeses. It didn't go well. For the last few years, she'd been reading Zola and Balzac, not confronting cheesemongers. After we left, she translated the exchange:

"Hello, sir."

"Hello, mademoiselle."

"I was hoping you might be able to help me. We'd like to buy a cheese, but we don't know very much. Could you please help me to buy a cheese made from the milk of a horse?"

The man who may or may not have been Pascal Trotté remained stony-faced. "That does not exist."

"Huh?"

"Perhaps you mean goat?"

Chuck laughed. "Of course, yes."

She got no laugh in return. "What are you looking for? What do you like?"

Chuck flustered.

"Perhaps a soft cheese?" he asked.

"Yes. Or a hard one."

"Maybe two?"

"That sounds good."

The man who may or may not have been Pascal Trotté selected a cheese and squeezed it.

"Oh," said Chuck.

He selected a second cheese.

"Is that one different from the other?"

"They're completely different."

They were completely different, but neither was a Livarot.

"Thank you so much. Looks great. Thank you for your help."

At this point, Chuck went to pay for our cheese and almost set down her purse on the store's pristine cutting board. This evoked the only facial expression we ever saw from the man who may or may not have been Pascal Trotté. It wasn't bonhomie. Its deadliness presaged the Livarot.

Chuck needed a few days. The mortification she felt over asking for horse cheese had to dwindle before she could go back to the shop, and she needed to go alone because, as she explained, my monolingual Americanness put too much pressure on her French. When she returned, she had a crinkle in her nose and a Livarot.

"Stinky" is not the right word for it. "Exhumed" might be. I have never seen a dug-up corpse, but I could now recognize the smell.

"I don't know if I can eat this," said Chuck, sinuses weeping.

Livarot, as far as I can tell, should be eaten in a windy, open field. It's made in the shape of a disc and, when halved, about the size of a clutch purse. It has a tacky, hatched skin that's as thick as a wet suit and pale peach in color. Inside the rind, it's globular and buttery. Here's the sketch Chuck drew before we ate it:

The French have nicknamed Livarot "The Little Colonel" because it comes circled in thin strips of raffia, but after tasting it, we dubbed it "The Gérard Depardieu" because it posed for us an enigma similar to the one surrounding the actor: Why do the French find so alluring what strikes us as raunchy, hulking, and nearly grotesque? The cheese tasted rotten, "really wretched." We wondered if we'd gotten a prime example.

And perhaps we hadn't. Perhaps the man who may or may not have been Pascal Trotté (we never got up the gumption to ask who was who in the store) had let an imperfect Livarot fall into the hands of an American who had strolled into his shop and asked, with what might have struck him as contemptuous ignorance about his life's work, for horse cheese? That hunch was probably wrong. All our other transactions with the various *fromagers* who may or may not have been Pascal Trotté resulted in superior cheeses, and, for the little we knew, maybe this was the way a Livarot was supposed to taste. Yet, whatever its quality, at least we'd learned its secret, which is the secret of all cheese: It tastes of life, but it also tastes of death.

"Cheese," says McCalman, "is nothing but spoiled milk," and Steven Jenkins, who wrote the massive *Cheese Primer* and helped bring artisanal cheese to America through Dean & DeLuca, agrees with him; he sums up the cheesemaking process as "controlled spoilage." Cheese, that is, achieves its flavor as milk goes from its most lively and life-giving to its inevitable end as rot. Along the way and through the care of its makers, cheese develops its unique character and, somewhere between its creation and putrefaction, attains its peak. So that stinkiness, that funkiness, that earthy, ashy tang you taste in even slightly aged cheeses, that flavor sends a half-conscious shiver to the deepest part of your being: *Memento mori*, remember you will die.

As you savor cheese, Eros and Thanatos dance on your tongue.

And that's why the Livarot loathed us as much as we loathed it.

We were in love, as anyone in Paris should be, and couldn't heed the tragic notes of any cheese, much less the requiem within the Livarot. We were too full of light and spent too much time luxuriating in the Tuileries and kissing on the Pont Neuf to fear the skull smiling at us through the spoiled milk. We courted Eros, and if you've ever caught the seminal whiff of a Saint-Marcellin or relished the cunnilingual mush of a Rocamadour, you know that cheese celebrates Eros in all its meanings. The death-stung Livarot must have found us wretched in its own way, as unserious and airy as Champagne bubbles.

Too airy, in fact, to take U.S. Customs and Border Patrol seriously.

At Logan Airport, as I stared at the mustaches in front of me, I tried to fathom how the cheeses in my bag could be illegal. The Comté, the Sainte-Maure, the Brique Ardéchoise, they were more alive than most people I knew. Could they really be confiscated? Incarcerated? Or—*Dieu* forbid—incinerated? The thought of it made me hate every whisker before me, then made me snicker.

"French cheeses are an emotional experience," Chuck had said when we were in the Marais, swooning over a Brie de Melun, and she's right.

In Paris, love is always right.

Tastes of Formaggio

he treasure we seek usually lies under our feet. We shoo away the golden goose to get off the farm. We ask the girl next door to help us woo the supermodel. We backpack through Tibet to find the self that belongs in Dubuque. We think life is a line, drawing us toward a far horizon, but it usually isn't. Usually it's a circle, and if we're lucky, we find ourselves back where we started, home again and wiser than we left.

Chuck and I came home from Paris unwise and cranky. No Aesop's fable or *It's a Wonderful Life* was going to convince us we hadn't been cast back into a cheese wasteland. America eats around nine billion pounds of cheese a year, but most of it amounts to the tasteless, rubberized fat that Domino's and Taco Bell slather on gummy nachos and greasy dough. Most of it, we shuddered, comes in shrink wrap. How could we be happy 3,446 miles from French cheese?

We tried. We looked at the cost of overnighting Camembert, but it was too much. We mapped routes from Cambridge to Montréal, where at least we could buy unpasteurized cheese, but it was too far. And we measured the time we'd have to wait until we could take another trip to Paris, but it was too long. We tried, but we figured we were doomed to our pasteurized, homogenized fate.

And then, after we had stopped trying and resigned ourselves to a life of Meximelts and double-crusts, we found our goose.

We were strolling down Brattle Street in Cambridge on a calm fall day, enjoying its colonial houses and the leaves that were just igniting in tangerine and rust. We turned a corner here, a corner there, our eyes caught by a blazing oak or lemony maple, and we wound up at the door of Formaggio Kitchen.

What, we wondered, lies inside a "Cheese" Kitchen?

Cheese isn't what you see when you walk in.

Instead you see an entire bakery's worth of baguettes and *pain poilâne levain* tucked behind the counter, where a chatty cashier with a pierced sternum or checkered driving cap is ringing up a Harvard professor with a sack of cornmeal or a roofer with a refillable mug and a brioche. Meanwhile, other customers waiting in line gaze on the delphinium, thistle, and flowering dogwood that the florist has arranged in her corner of the store or they sneak a locally grown raspberry from its carton.

Since you're in the way, you shuffle aside, but as soon as you do, the Darjeeling and Oolong teas stop you. As do the Giamaica Bababudans Peaberry coffee beans and Marcona almonds and rambutan. And you can't not check out the coolers, where you find seaweed butter and duck eggs alongside Russian Imperial Stout and Duchy Originals Organic English Ale. And that's only the start of the beers, so you promise yourself you'll circle back to the Belgian lambic and then pick out one of the Armenian cucumbers you spot among the farm-fresh vegetables.

You move on. The next room is smaller and more stuffed than the first. You could almost skip across it, except that you'd miss the rhododendron honey and the preserves made from cipollini onions. You'd also miss the truffles and burnt caramel toffee, not to mention the ginger-almond teacake that's been baked in the kitchen on-site. Saliva builds in your mouth, and you think how unjust it is that cows get four stomachs, especially when you see entire Taleggios and huge hunks of Dutch Boerenkaas set out on a gray marble slab for you to taste.

A moment later and mouth full, you look past the bottles of Saumur, Lambrusco, and Grüner Veltliner that fill the shelf of "Everyday Drinking Wines" into the last room, where Holy Mary, Mother of God, you spy a pile of cheese as high as yourself.

Formaggio calls it the "wall."

You stumble toward it and you stare. It's gorgeous. And it's just part of the three hundred different cheeses that now surround you. You see cheeses inside cases, cheeses stacked on cases, cheeses so massive and sturdy that they get used as cases on which to display more cheeses.

Drawn to a Nostrale di Elva or Wensleydale, you begin reading the hand-lettered descriptions. You learn about a cheese from Portugal called Cabra Pimento that's rubbed with paprika, and a cheese from Graubünden that Maria Mayer makes by collecting milk from five farms in her Swiss village, and, as you read on, you realize that whoever wrote these signs is on a first-name basis with cheesemakers in Piedmont and Valencia, the Loire Valley, and the Swiss Alps. You're so absorbed that you hardly glance at the shelves of spices and wine behind you or the rows of balsamic vinegar and olive oils to the side of you. You also miss the olives themselves, which gleam in their jars like wet jewels or chunks of blown glass, and the entire legs of Jamón Ibérico that dangle above you, hooves intact.

You're too excited. You've discovered the entire world of cheese in a single room. You're also overwhelmed. How will you choose one? Or two? Or twenty? Your cheese know-how feels woefully inadequate. What do you do?

I toyed with the idea of tasting our way through the entire store, an ounce or two, a cheese or two, at a time.

The math dissuaded Chuck. Three hundred tastes, even in two-ounce portions, adds up to about thirty-eight pounds of cheese. Chuck has a habit of rapping her fist against her chest like a centurion or sinning monk whenever I try to plug our arteries, and she began drumming out a steady, thumping rhythm. I might, had I known it then, have pointed out that thirty-eight pounds of cheese is how much the average Swede eats in a year, which is five pounds more than Americans and twenty pounds less than the French, but I didn't and I didn't mind. If the Saint-Maure Belgique I was eyeing tasted as luscious as its creamy color, I would want more than two ounces.

So, I proposed we choose at random. Fate had led us to Formaggio, perhaps it would lead us to the right cheese. Chuck nixed this idea too. She worried that choosing one cheese would cut us off from the 299 others.

"Even if we get ten," she said flatly, "we only get ten."

Here I need to pause and explain Chuck's approach to making choices. Most of us accept that, in choosing a meal at a restaurant or a movie at the video store, we must make our choice at the exclusion of others. We can't have the steak frites and the braised lamb. We can't watch *The Philadelphia Story* and *Amélie*, at least not at once. Most of us accept that, although we choose it with a sigh, we must choose a road to travel by.

Not Chuck. For her, two roads are a torment. She dreads when the waiter returns, for the fourth time, to take our order ("We're not quite ready yet"), and I've followed her back and forth across Cambridge so she could decide between what seemed to me identical pairs of black flats. It isn't greed. Chuck isn't Imelda Marcos or Carrie Bradshaw, wanting everything. In the end, she refuses to buy the flats ("The cost-to-style ratio is off"), and we browse for hours in Hollywood Video before she decides we should leave empty-handed. No, it's that Chuck doesn't want to miss out. She sees the possibilities, all the possibilities, and doesn't want to waste any of them. Life is infinitely rich, and she's curious, not only about what it offers, but also about what *else* it offers.

"How can you choose," she'll explain, "if you don't know what else you're not choosing?"

Formaggio offered Chuck a lot of else. And as I watched her going doe-eyed, I realized we could spend years in here, looking at cheeses, debating their potential, only to head home and eat hummus on saltines rather than taste a Queso Azul de Valdeón from Leon or a Tomme Geante from Auvergne.

Chuck and I needed a plan. So, I resolved to create a cheese-selecting system, one that would save Chuck from the agony of choosing, me from the hummus, and both of us from angina. I would order this cheese chaos before us. Somehow, I would figure out Formaggio.

Start simply, I told myself, and since I couldn't start unwrapping cheeses and didn't yet know that the cheesemongers would generously unwrap them for me so I could sample them, I started with their names.

Right away, I learned I didn't even know the words for "cheese." What distinguished a *kaas* from a *käse*, a *cacio* from a *queso*, a *Bergkäse* from *Jurakäse* from *Försterkäse* from *Weichkäse*? Maybe if I could spot "cheese" in the cheese names, I could focus on the more descriptive words? Maybe then I wouldn't ask a cheesemonger, "What kind of cheese is this käse?"

I cracked the dictionaries.

It turns out that most of the words we use for cheese, the ones that come from Europe anyway, have their origins in Latin. The Romans called cheese *caseus*. It's the word from which we get "casein," the main protein that's in milk and cheese, as well as "caseophile," a lover of cheese. "Caseus," in turn, has a root that runs back to the very beginning, to what linguists call the Proto-Indo-European language. Between six and ten thousand years ago, this theory goes, the ancestors of those folks now speaking in Europe, India, and much of Asia used the syllable "kwat." By "kwat," they meant "to ferment" or "to become sour," as milk does when it becomes cheese, and "kwat" eventually became the Latin word "caseus."

The other Latin word that the Romans used for cheese is *formaticum*. Around the time Rome began building its Empire, its soldiers needed cheese made in a "form, shape, or mold" so that they could carry it with them. When you marched off to war against Germania, you carried your sword, your shield, your memories of boyhood, and your molded cheese. The rise of "formaticum" tells us that cheesemaking became a regular and widespread practice in Rome.

From these two words, "caseus" and "formaticum," you can trace most of the big names for cheese. Just keep in mind that when Rome and Germania clashed, so did their languages. I don't know whether the Romans brought cheese to the Germanic people or the Germanic people eventually began using a Roman word for the cheese they were making before the Romans arrived. Whatever happened, "caseus" became the Germanic "kasjus," and once you get to the Germanic languages, you've reached the origin of today's German, Dutch, and English.

And, since you're reading in English, I'll mention that the first instance we have of the word that eventually became "cheese" occurs just before or just after the first millennium, in the glossary for a book of dialogues written by the abbot

Ælfric. "Cyse" appears in the phrase "cyse and buteran," and from this Old English "cyse" comes the Middle English "chese," and from it and a few hundred years, we get our "cheese."

Here's how it all looks:

SAYING "CHEESE"

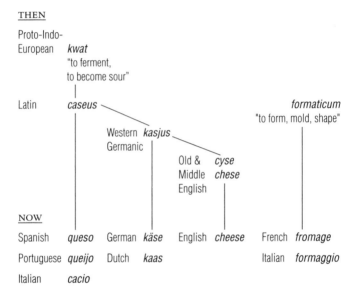

THEN

Proto-Indo-European *kwat*
"to ferment, to become sour"

Latin *caseus* — formaticum
"to form, mold, shape"

Western *kasjus*
Germanic

Old & *cyse*
Middle *chese*
English

NOW

Spanish *queso*　German *käse*　English *cheese*　French *fromage*

Portuguese *queijo*　Dutch *kaas*　Italian *formaggio*

Italian *cacio*

As I looked over the history of "cheese" for the last 6,000 years, I felt brainy. I began hoping someone at work or on the street would ask me about *cacioricotta* and *fromage blanc* and *boerenkaas*, so I could say, "Cheese, cheese, cheese."

I was a one-word polyglot.

*　*　*

Unfortunately, one word wouldn't do.

I needed at least four. Four because, in addition to "cheese," I needed three more words to distinguish the three basic kinds of cheese: cow, sheep, and goat, the animals that give the cheesemaking milk. (I left out buffalos and, for Pascal's and Chuck's sake, horses.) Sure, I could say "cheese," but I had to start systematizing it.

So, I climbed up Babel's Tower once again and came down with a whole bunch of barnyard trios:

THE THREE CHEESES
(SANS BUFFALO AND HORSE)

ENGLISH	GERMAN	DUTCH	SPANISH
cow	kuh	koe	vaca
goat	ziege	geit	cabra
sheep	schafe	schapen	oveja

	PORTUGUESE	FRENCH	ITALIAN
	vaca	vache	mucca or vacca
	cabra	chèvre	capra
	carneiros	brebis	pecora

That, for me, was a lot of words. I stink at languages and still battle with post-traumatic stress from high-school Spanish. ("No sé! No sé!") If East Asia began making cheese, I'd have to resort to moo, bah, and bleat.

Still, with my small cheese vocabulary, I could travel through Europe asking for formaggio and make sense of a

Ziegenkäse. I couldn't say much, but I could say what counted: cow cheese, goat cheese, sheep cheese. I had a start.

Then, I had a headache.

Once you get beyond the three milks, cheese gets complicated. I wanted it to be simple. I wanted there to be some Rosetta Stone of curd that would allow me to decode and classify every cheese in Formaggio's wall, and, at first, I thought finding one would be easy. Every cheese guidebook and Web site seemed to have one, but as I studied all the cheese systems created by mongers and makers, I saw that, while any one of them looks right by itself, taken together they resembled the system invented by Jorge Luis Borges in a description he gives of animals. The description appears in a fictional Chinese encyclopedia called the *Heavenly Emporium of Benevolent Knowledge:*

> In its distant pages it is written that animals are divided into (a) those that belong to the emperor; (b) embalmed ones; (c) those that are trained; (d) suckling pigs; (e) mermaids; (f) fabulous ones; (g) stray dogs; (h) those that are included in this classification; (i) those that tremble as if they were mad; (j) innumerable ones; (k) those drawn with a very fine camel's-hair brush; (l) et cetera; (m) those that have just broken the flower vase; (n) those that at a distance resemble flies.

Borges's system spoofs systematization itself. It orders things (a, b, c . . .) that defy order ("et cetera") and cleverly reminds us that the world won't fit into the tidy systems we find on Wikipedia or in *Britannica*. It shakes up, as the philosopher Michel Foucault puts it, the ways "in which we are accustomed to tame the wild profusion of existing things."

Cheese, in its abundance and variety, is wildly profuse. The more I tried to systematize it, the more I saw it was like the animal who has just broken the flower vase, wonderfully untamable.

So, instead of going through another cheese guide, I imagined how a less clever Borges might describe cheese in the *Earthly Hodgepodge of Dairy Wisdom*:

> In its milk-stained pages it is written that cheese is divided into (a) those wrapped in leaves or wood; (b) fresh ones; (c) those that are hard; (d) unpressed curds; (e) blues; (f) pasteurized ones; (g) natural rinds; (h) those that are excluded from this classification; (i) those introduced to *Lactococcus lactis*; (j) innumerable ones; (k) fatty; (l) those with a Protected Designation of Origin; (m) et cetera; (n) those cooked at a temperature of 48–56°C; (o) those you happen to really, really like.

"We could just ask for help."

Chuck's sensible statement incensed me. Ask? If I asked a monger about which cheese to buy, I might as well ask a dentist for help with a cavity. Didn't she see that I could figure out Formaggio—and formaggio—for myself?

Besides, at the moment Chuck questioned me, I had already assembled a cheese library that went back to Osbert Burdett's 1935 *A Little Book of Cheese* ("The simple hope of the following pages . . . is to aid the reader in the choice of cheese") and up to the latest edition of Slow Food's guide to *Italian Cheese* ("A comprehensive catalog of produce from an incredible variety of landscapes and environments, of animal breeds and production techniques") and I was, I was sure, close to success.

Admittedly, my system had flaws. It still couldn't tell you who made the cheese, whether it came from a small farm, for example, or a factory. And it couldn't tell you a cheese's official status, whether it had a legally protected name and origin as the A.O.C. cheeses do in France and the D.O.P. cheeses do in Italy. I also hadn't included the blue cheeses, which seem to be a category in themselves, and there were other categories, such as curd-cutting or fat content, that I didn't know then and probably more categories that I don't know now.

I had, however, included a lot. How much did the cheesemakers heat or cook the milk as they were making it? Did they press the curds to expel the whey and harden the cheese or did they let the curds remain moist and the cheese become soft? Did they wash the rind with a salt solution to flavor it, did they introduce it to mold and make it bloom as Brie does, or did they just let it develop naturally? My system made sense of all these differences.

Here's how it looked, at its best, before I knew that no system could account for every cheese:

ERIC'S INHERENTLY FAULTY BUT
SOMEWHAT HELPFUL CHEESE SYSTEM

MILK	CURD	TEXTURE	RIND	AGE
uncooked	unpressed	soft	natural	fresh
semicooked	semipressed	semisoft	bloomy	semi-aged
cooked	pressed	hard	washed	aged

The problem was that, even if my system weren't inherently faulty and even if it were wholly helpful, it would be weird to use. I might bristle at Chuck's suggestion of asking a monger for help, but would I really swagger up to one and ask for a semicooked, semipressed, semisoft, semi-aged, bloomy-rind cheese please? Would that really give me more cheese cachet than crying for help like a frustrated toddler?

In the end, I cried.

Formaggio and formaggio were too vast, and, as much fun as system-making can be, it can't compare to eating cheese. So Chuck and I walked back into the store, up to the wall, and asked a monger, "What's good?"

David helped us. With his cropped hair and trimmed beard, he has the posture and look of a fighter pilot. Chuck and I learned later that he's trained as a professional chef and possesses a demonic ability to pick wines. David usually begins by saying, "What I would recommend is . . ." He's never pushy, and you'd never know he's so talented if you didn't push him to push you. (Chuck now interrogates David as though she's a homicide cop: "Are you sure this is the cheese we want?

What are you hiding? What aren't you telling us?!") After some back and forth, in which we displayed our cluelessness, David brought out a Robiola di Roccaverano Fresco, a creamy goat cheese from Piedmont that chews of citrus and sunshine, and we tasted it right there, in tiny plastic spoonfuls. It was good. Very good.

From that moment on, our cheese-buying system came down to asking David, or Kurt, or Gemma, "What's good?"

And that's the question you want to ask, whether you're at Formaggio or your local cheese shop, because the monger is the one who knows. Cheese, in a wall of 300 or a display of thirty, is always changing, aging, attaining its peak or falling from it, and it's the monger who cares for it, who tastes it day in and day out. And that knowledge lets a monger take whatever preferences you might give—a texture you like, a taste you don't, a dish you're cooking, a mood you're in—and find you a match.

It's the monger, not the system, who knows what's good.

And what if there's no David in your neighborhood? One appendix in this book can help you locate a monger online. Another suggests our best cheese finds, many of which came from the great mongers we've met and others which came from luck, happenstance, serendipity, from the fun of adventuring outside a system.

A Tomme at Twig Farm

To call Michael Lee a cheesemaker feels like a lie.

If you met him on his farm in West Cornwall, Vermont, and saw his sun-worn Red Sox cap and rustic smile, you'd think he'd sprung from the local tunbridge soil. But you'd also notice his barn was painted a funky chartreuse and you'd glimpse the abstract tattoo on his bicep and you'd start wondering if maybe he wasn't a displaced Soho hipster.

Later, as you strolled with him through patches of juniper, goldenrod, trefoil, and clover and tasted the stems he casually plucked and handed to you as he described western Vermont's wind and rain patterns or its limestone, you'd think he was a horti-geo-meteorologist. But when you squatted alongside his goat Crab Cake and followed his index finger as he detailed the ideal goat haunch or explained the benefits of dehorning kids in late winter to avoid flies, you'd decide he was an expert in animal husbandry.

Until, that is, you listened to him enthuse about the molecular separation of curds and whey, which would make you think he was a chemist. Though when you entered his aging cave and felt the ammonia hit your nose and marveled at the hundreds of cheeses lining the walls in neat military rows, you'd wonder if he wasn't something of a mad scientist, creating moldy little monsters in his underground lab. After all, you'd watch him work with a strange mixture called "morge" and you'd hear him address each cheese as "you."

But Michael Lee *is* a cheesemaker. And if you ask him what it takes to make cheese, he won't say you need a working knowledge of ecology, gastronomy, veterinary medicine, or any of the other subjects he slides into with ease. He'll say you need one thing: "Imagination."

"Tradition" is the answer you'd expect.

Read up on any celebrated cheese, a Comté or Parmigiano-Reggiano, and you're likely to learn about medieval shepherds pounding up mountains or farmers tucked away in remote villages, making the cheese of their fathers' fathers' fathers. In these stories, tradition means quality. Tradition means that a cheese comes from generations of cheesemakers who have refined their recipe over centuries until it's reached perfection. Tradition also means trouble if, like Michael Lee, you've been making cheese since 2005. A few years isn't much of a start, much less a tradition. Not that Michael isn't up for tradition's demands. He's looking toward a life on Twig Farm.

"I like to joke that I've got a thirty-year plan here," he said in an interview that took place right after he started. "I'm going to do this for thirty years, then I'm either going to pass it on or hang it up."

Joke or no joke, his plan impresses me. I can't imagine a job I'd tick off in years ("One down," laughs Michael, "twenty-nine to go"), but that's his point: A cheesemaker thrives on imagination. And Michael imagined the whole of his operation before he began it. He imagined the design of the house, the barn, the cave, and, even though he insists that he makes only three cheeses—a tomme, a washed rind, and a groovy semisoft he calls "square cheese"—when you look around his aging shelves, you'll spot all sorts of experiments tucked away in the corners; these are cheeses he's still imagining into being. The latest of them is the "fuzzy wheel," a cheese he's based on his washed rind, but instead of washing it, he lets it grow a fuzzy gray mold. After a few weeks, it looks like a leukemia-ridden cat. It's delicious.

The fuzzy wheel was what inspired Chuck and me to visit Michael at Twig Farm. We had tried it at Formaggio, where Michael once worked and where it bested the other American goat cheeses we sampled, from Maine to Oregon. It has a bright burst up front that rounds into rocky earth. That complexity is rare enough in an American cheese, but the fuzzy wheel also has a singular taste, which is what I kept saying, "It's so singular," because I couldn't pinpoint what makes it singular. I pestered Chuck for an answer.

"What makes it so singular?"

"Not sure," Chuck thoughtfully chewed.

"Here," I said, handing her my piece, "try it again."

Chuck tried it again. And again, until she'd swiped my fuzzy wheel, but we never figured out what it was. Now we know. Michael's cheese is untraditional. It tastes fresh, unfettered, uniquely its own. You might say it's imaginative.

* * *

"What's your shoe size?"

Our first words from Michael weren't about tradition, imagination, or the complexities of cheese, but footwear.

Michael has a lot of shoes. He has rubber clogs for his cave, squeaky boots for his cheesemaking, shitkickers for his pastures. We must have seen him change shoes seven or eight times while we were with him. He even has shoes for fixing lunch. The shoes make sense once you see the care he takes to keep his milk clean and cheese pure. His barn has swept corners, his curd knives gleam, and the concrete walls of his cave look freshly poured, despite the dank air. Michael makes surgeons look like slobs.

We didn't know that yet, but we dutifully gave him our shoe sizes and put on the clogs he keeps for guests. We then scrubbed up and followed him into the cave, where he set us to work turning cheese.

"You can do the least damage this way," he assured us.

Chuck shot me a look. She worries in worst cases ("What if, when I'm in the cave, I sneeze?"), so I knew that as soon as Michael cast our work as potential damage, she'd start fretting. I nodded at her, with more confidence than I felt, and, with a crinkled brow, she began turning the square cheese. I got the tommes.

Cheese needs turning because, as it ages, its moisture sinks. Turning it keeps its texture and taste balanced. I found the work repetitive—down the rows you go, making tops bottoms and bottoms tops—but not boring. You're squatting, craning, and torquing to reach the cheeses at the backs of the shelves, so you're happily aware of your body. You also get to see the way a cheese ages over several weeks, almost in time-lapse photography. Some cheeses splotch and mottle, others grow uniformly dark, but all of them could be *objets d'art* and, taken together, create an installation you might find at MoMA. They feel cool, too. The tommes are sticky and dense, like diving bricks. And your hands gradually develop their own layer of mold as you move from cheese to cheese. Before long, you're leaving your prints on the rinds.

And your rhythmic turning, along with the cave's dreamy light, the whir of its cooling fan, and its ammonia-laden air, all lead to a state of mind in which you want to wax about what it might mean to make an imaginative cheese, even after you've finished turning your tommes and Michael gives you your next job.

"Use this squeegee and work along the floor, wiping up the cheese goobers."

As I wiped up the cheese goobers, by which Michael meant the bits of cheese that come off the rinds as you wash them, I came to this conclusion: If you're an imaginative cheese-maker, you might have mixed feelings about tradition.

You'd value tradition, of course, and you'd certainly need it. From where else would you get the knowledge to make your cheese? But tradition also might stifle you, not because you'd want to defy it and start making "imaginative" cheeses in zucchini skins or out of badger milk, but because tradition wants to preserve the past. Tradition asks you to inherit what's known, maintain it, and carry it forward, whereas imagination wants to create. Imagination asks you to discover what's still possible. If you're an imaginative cheesemaker, tradition might cramp your ability to make cheese.

I learned later that I'm not the first to see this tension. In *The Taste of Place: A Cultural Journey into Terroir*, Amy Trubek explains how a view of food that prizes tradition often "leads to a nostalgia for the past and difficulties in imagining the future." This problem becomes particularly bad for Americans, since, as Oscar Wilde once observed, our lack of tradition is our oldest tradition. Here's how Trubek puts it:

> According to this view the lack of a long agrarian tradition in the United States, and the swift transition from small-scale peasant farms to large commodity farms, dooms us to a long, slow walk toward *terroir*; only the passage of time will give us the customs and know-how necessary to really taste place.

Terroir, in this view, emerges only after an eon or two of tradition has draw it from the earth. And that does sound like doom if, like Michael, you have only twenty-nine years to make cheese or, like me, as much time to eat it.

Against this doom, there's hope. Rather than viewing place and tradition as inextricably linked, you can view place as a good in itself, whether or not a given place has a tradition. This view gets argued for and celebrated in books such as Trubek's and magazines such as *Edible Chicago* or *Missoula*. It informs the work of groups such as Farm Fresh to You, Community Supported Agriculture, and the Vermont Fresh Network. And it inspires the foodies at your farmer's market down

the street, who'll sing its watchword—"Local!"—as they show
you their lumpy heirloom tomatoes or leafy kale. Locavores
like Trubek triumph place, but a place doesn't have to have an
established past. Focus on local alone and you can have new
farms and new fields. You can have *terroir* without tradition.

You can also have imagination. If your aim is to capture
a *terroir*, especially in a place where no one has tried before,
you'll need your imagination. How else will you find the
flavors in America's tradition-poor soil? How else will you
accomplish your aim?

"I want a cheese that reflects a place, that comes from a
specific place," says Michael. "The more specific I can make
it, the happier I'll be."

He should be happy. His cheese tastes and looks like western
Vermont. You might mistake his square cheese for a lichen-
spotted stone that's been pulled from the New Haven River,
and his tomme has a rind that looks like schist. Even in black
and white, this image isn't far off.

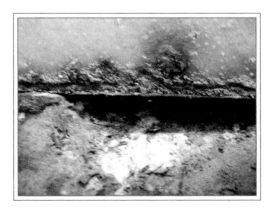

As for taste, both start brightly, the square cheese with a yogurty burst, the tomme with a lemon tang. Then both move to the ground. The square cheese gives you black pepper and green bean before it finishes in gravel, and the tomme sighs into animal and dirt. For cheeses so full of *terroir*, they're surprisingly unbucolic. They find the bounty in Vermont's rocky landscape and coax out its hard flavors.

"They're cheeses that comfort you in your solitude," said Chuck, an inward look in her eye.

It's true. Even though Michael hosts picnics for a local church and attends town meetings (he wanted to hear the debate about a new dog ordinance) and even though he has a young son named Carter who takes swimming lessons and a hip partner named Emily who handles the business side of Twig Farm, you can easily picture him standing on a windswept crag in the Green Mountains, his goat herd below him, gray sky above, and under his arm, his tomme. He and it, elemental and alone.

I doubt Michael would agree with this picture, but I don't think he'd mind it. He's very nonchalant about how people respond to his cheese. He'd just smile when Chuck or I asked a dumb question. ("Is that mold?") And when I mentioned the upcoming competition held by the American Cheese Society, which are the Oscars of American cheese, he looked at me quizzically. I had to explain that I was talking—"you know"—about the competition he had entered before, the one at which—"remember?"—his cheeses had won prestigious awards in the Farmstead Goat Cheese category.

"Oh, yeah," he recalled, "I'll probably send a few again this year."

Michael isn't out for glory. He says he makes cheese because he wants to eat it and sells the rest. That's obviously true, but it's also his stock line. Something he said in the cave as he was washing rinds struck me as less stock and more true. He was telling us how he likes that cheese unites so many disparate things. The land, the goats, the milk, the season, all of them and all his work come together in the moment when you eat his cheese. He likes that impermanence: that it's there, that you eat it, that it's gone, that you're nourished. I knew he was once a painter and sculptor, so I asked him about audience. What did he want us to experience as we ate his cheese?

He stared at the wet cheese in his hand and said, "I just want it to exist."

That existence is precarious.

Ten months out of the year, Michael can't miss a day of work. The goats need daily attention when they're giving milk, and with milk comes the need to make and care for cheese. No one else knows how to do everything on the farm that Michael does, and he can't afford an assistant. So, if he gets sick or hurt, that's it. His cheese won't exist.

That puts a lot of pressure on Michael, and the more Chuck and I saw how much work he does, the more we were amazed he wasn't bone-weary and cross. We wouldn't have lasted a day.

Only once did we see a hint of the strain Michael feels. Right before we left, he took us into the pastures to meet his goats. He calls them his girls ("Where's my goats? Where's my girls?"), and his girls have as much affection for him as he does for them. Indeed, they have affection to spare. Agatha, Brandeis, and Esther took turns butting their foreheads into our butts. That made chatting difficult, especially for Chuck, who didn't do well with how much and how freely goats piss and shit.

I did, however, manage to ask Michael if he always worked with the end in mind. When he was in the pasture or milking parlor, did he imagine how his work would influence the final taste of his cheese?

"You can think about it that way if you want," he sighed. He wasn't smiling. He was feeding a stalk of grass to Crab Cake, almost talking to her, and waving off black flies, "But mostly it's about what's next. It's about getting it all done."

"So, what's next?" I asked.

His smiled returned, all teeth. "Today?" he said and shrugged at a far thicket. "Today's bushwhacking!"

Foggy

San Francisco has always fascinated me. And not always in a good way.

I should say I hadn't been there since I rode a tricycle, so its allure arose more from the city's history, as home of *The Birds* and the Beats, Haight-Ashbury and the Castro, and even more from the secondhand stories I'd hear from friends who'd gone to visit and returned with smooth, featureless faces.

"What the hell happened to your face?!" I'd ask on a bleak Monday morning in Boston, as I jammed a Dunkin' Donut in my mouth and scrawled meetings in my calendar.

"Nothing," they'd say. "I'm relaxed."

"Relaxed?"

"Yeah, relaxed."

"What's that like?" By now, I'd stopped scrawling.

"You gotta go to San Francisco," they'd say. "I'm moving there."

And they would. They'd move away and leave me with meetings and cruller crumbs. Sometimes they'd send postcards about lush farmers markets that take place "*all year long*" or *taquerias* "right around the corner" where you can feast better than any white-tablecloth joint in Boston and for four bucks. Their East Coast angst had vanished. They were "laid back," they were "chill," they stressed me out.

I put off visiting. I didn't really want to undergo the San Fran Effect, did I? It seemed cultish. Everyone who moved there tried to convince everyone else to move there. In San Francisco, some other self, some San Fran me, might emerge. What if I went and found a me that was calm and insufferable or what if I came back and couldn't handle the former me that was waiting here? I made excuses. "My calendar," I'd write back. "Remember when you had a calendar?"

Still, the fascination grew, and not always in a bad way. What, I'd wonder, would life be like if I didn't wake at three in the morning and worry about my to-do list? And what, exactly, is involved in chilling?

So, when the chance came to visit San Francisco and try some West Coast cheese, I faced my fear of tranquility and flew into the setting sun.

It was late December, ugly weather, which I believed would protect me from the city's witchery. I would act the Arthurian knight. I would find, as though it were the Grail, the taste of the West Coast. In cheese.

At first, it seemed the West Coast must taste like derelicts.

I arrived in San Francisco at night, the city ablaze, and, on the van ride from the airport, spotted Market Street and a picturesque trolley. I felt revved, ready to strike out. I expected to see fresh root vegetables and farmstead yogurt on every amiable corner.

Instead, I saw massage parlors. Massage parlors, liquor stores, and squalor. My hotel, I later learned, was situated in the Tenderloin, a neighborhood famous for its seedy one-bedroom apartments, Dumpsters, and disproportionately high murder rate, and although the methadone addicts and drunks I met were eager to assist me in my search for the nearest artisanal cheese shop, I didn't feel as though San Francisco was fulfilling my expectations.

"You would do that," said Damion, somewhat exasperated when he picked me up in a Zipcar the next day, and I told him about a zombie-eyed guy who tried to hit me with a rusty shovel.

"The Tenderloin is the worst part of the city."

Damion and his wife are friends from Cambridge who were sucked up by San Francisco two years ago, and of everyone I'd known who'd undergone the San Fran Effect, Damion struck me as the most unlikely. Damion comes from Manhattan, muscles his way through Angkor Wat and Slovenia as though he's wintering in St. Barts, publishes five books in a year and reads nine dozen more, picks up French in a week so he can interview at U.N.E.S.C.O. in Paris, but ends up moving to Portugal instead, so he can assemble an edition of Thoreau's journals for *New York Review Books*, translate Rilke, and send you charming e-mails about eating canned sardines from a quaint local merchant and overcoming food poisoning. Damion is brilliant and good and sometimes a little prickly, but Damion is not chill.

So, I took comfort in the fact that Damion, now an ardent San Fran evangelist living in "the perfect apartment" in the Mission, could still get riled as I told him about a few of the locals I'd met. Maybe living in San Francisco didn't mean you lost all of your East Coast vim.

"There's Bob." I pointed at a man wearing two winter coats and no pants. "I helped Bob with bus fare."

"We're going past Layfette Park," Damion said, ignoring me and aiming the Zipcar up Van Ness Avenue.

"And that's Sam." I pointed again. "Sam wanted to show me his foot rash."

"Nicolas Cage lives there," Damion continued.

"And that guy pushing the broken television, that's another Sam."

"So does Danielle Steel."

"Danielle Steel?" A shiver spindled in my chest.

"Yep," said Damion, smiling. He knew I was impressed. "Some serious dog walking happens in Lafayette Park."

I wanted to stop and soak in the aura of a writer who has published 75 novels, which have been translated into 28 languages, adapted into 22 movies and television shows, been on the *New York Times* Best-Seller List for 390 consecutive weeks, and sold 550 million copies.

Damion didn't. He wanted to show me Golden Gate Park, the Presidio, and the Pacific Ocean. He was right, of course, and after a longing glance at Danielle Steel's stately mansion and a few overgroomed poodles, we zipped on.

The next afternoon, however, I hoofed back to Lafayette Park so I could get in my Danielle Steel aura-soak.

On the way, I stopped by Cheese Plus, a cheese shop on Polk Street in Russian Hill, where I asked a robust, full-cheeked monger for "a cheese that captured the essence of the West Coast." This question would become my refrain. He quizzically puffed out his cheeks, and we entered into a back-and-forth that ended with me leaving the store carrying half a goat cheese made by Sally Jackson on a small farm in Oroville, Washington, and a bottle of Le Freak Ale from a brewery in San Diego named Green Flash, after the light that can appear for an instant when the sun changes colors at sunrise or sunset.

A few minutes later, I was plunked on a park bench in front of Danielle Steel's mansion, the grandest in the city, eating cheese with my fingers and sucking down Le Freak from a paper bag.

Maybe it was the afternoon sunlight glinting off of the limestone façade of the mansion, which sugar-baron Adolph Spreckels built in 1913 for his wife, Alma, a nude model who eventually became "Big Alma," the "Great Grand-mother of San Francisco," long before Danielle Steel moved in. Or maybe it was the high, exclusive hedges behind which Danielle Steel clacked out her stories on a 1946 Olympia typewriter. Or maybe it was the cawing of the inky black crows that shuttled from the mansion's balustrade to the cypress branches above me as I smacked on Sally Jackson's cheese. Maybe it was the ale. Whatever it was, I realized that the best way to taste a cheese is to follow the story it tells.

By story, I don't mean "Once upon a time there were these curds . . ." or that a cheese contains the story of its making, though that's also true.

Instead, I mean story as structure, a particular sequence of events used by storytellers as long ago as Sophocles and as recently as Danielle Steel. Aristotle defined this structure just before Alexander conquered the world, but it's so well-known that your ninth-grade English teacher might have chalked it on the blackboard. Every story, according to Aristotle and Mr. Hendricks, should have a

BEGINNING   MIDDLE   END

It's simple, but most storytellers admit it's hard to fulfill. Think of all the movies you've seen with flashy openings that devolve into bum-punishers or the novels you've dropped midway through. Stories with satisfying beginnings, middles, and ends are surprisingly rare.

What does this structure have to do with cheese?

The answer came as I tasted Sally Jackson's cheese. My mouth was a mess of flavors. I tasted sour, probably from the grape leaves in which the cheese was wrapped. I tasted yogurt, probably from the goat milk. I tasted smooth and thought, "How can you *taste* smooth?" I tried to piece it together, but my sensations toppled over one another, with neither shape nor sense.

Then, in a Le Freaky green flash, the spatial-temporal presence of Danielle Steel inspired me to make sense of all my cheesy sensations by shaping them into a story. Cheese begins with specific flavors and textures, and, as you chew, those flavors and textures alter, until at last they end, usually leaving some sort of aftertaste. You might say tasting cheese has a beginning, a middle, and an end. Experts will talk about a cheese's "start" and "finish," but what about its in-between? You can better capture all its tastes by thinking of cheese as a story.

Take, for example, a bite of Sally Jackson's goat cheese. Here's the story it unfolds:

BEGINNING

Zing! A spike of sticky, slightly crumbly grape-leaf sourness and goat-cheese tang hints of the ape house.

MIDDLE

Ahh . . . Grape-leaf and curd merge in a soothing, delicious mush, though a gentle bite remains, a lover's nip.

END

Whither hast thou gone, my love? Yogurt and saliva linger in a salty note, not unpleasant, but too near to nothing.

A Danielle Steel romance it isn't, but following a cheese's story lets you relish the flavors you're tasting in its milky twists and mushy turns. And if words aren't how you like your stories, you can sketch your taste experience as though your mouth were hooked up to a cardiograph.

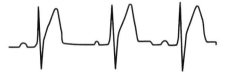

BEGINNING

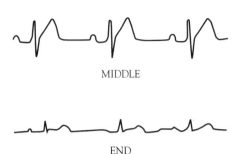

MIDDLE

END

You can see how Sally Jackson's cheese pounds at you at first, in spikes of flavor, but then settles down and pulses dulcetly on your palate. It's delicious. Its beats of grape-leaf and yogurt tang transport you, and you can see why it's won a bunch of awards. Until its end, when it gutters out and dies. So you revive it with another bite, and another, because it's so good in the middle, and with each new bite, its story starts again.

Eat a cheese, and your mouth becomes a stage, a screen, a *New York Times* Best Seller by Danielle Steel. Chew, and a cheese tells you its story.

And I wanted to hear the story of the West Coast.

Damion kept insisting that we should go to the Bi-Rite Market around the corner from his perfect apartment. I resisted. Bi-Rite sounded too close to all those icky, misspelled stores I grew up around—Pick 'n Save, Thriftway, ShopRite—and I didn't want to get my West Coast cheese in the San Fran equivalent of a Quik Mart.

I was wrong. Bi-Rite isn't a cheese shop, but a cornucopia of everything delicious—baskets of luscious pineapples, bunches of sweet carrots, sashimi grade Ahi tuna, you name it. At Bi-Rite, and with no small "told you" from Damion, I saw the fecundity of the West Coast. Here was a corner store you'd move around the corner for. The cheeses, though fewer in number, were as unique and inviting as those in any good cheese shop. And our monger, if he was a monger, got into my question about the essence of the West Coast. He helped us sort through the cheeses, then started pulling local wines. We were in foodie Eden, with our own bearded and ball-capped angel named Patrick to help us pick its fruits.

Later, in Damion's perfect apartment, as we were drinking one of Patrick's picks, Damion averred that what's West Coast about West Coast cheese is that you don't need a cheese shop. West Coast cheese is just part of the West Coast's widespread, oceanic, always-in-season abundance, and Damion is rite.

Humboldt Fog may be the most beautiful cheese I've ever seen.

Its outer rim has the texture of a frozen sea. Rough, foam-colored wavelets crest from it, and beneath them lies a greenish gray ash that hints of ocean before a storm. Its top has a hatched, perky pattern and could pass for a frosted pastry. If you were thumb-sized, you'd want to throw yourself onto it and make snow angels.

Once you slice it open, it reveals more beauties. Just beneath the rind, the cheese has broken down in a layer of off-white goo that surrounds the firmer, finely ribbed *pâte*. And the *pâte* blinds you. It's the same stark white as the rind, except for a layer of ash, razor thin, that runs through it and gives shape to all that whiteness. If you smeared it on a canvas, you might mistake it for an abstract painting by Agnes Martin or an albino Mark Rothko. You might also shove candles into it and serve it at a birthday.

Humboldt Fog gets its name from the fog that rolls into Humboldt Bay, which is close to where it's made, about 300 miles north of San Francisco. The bays must link the two places, because Patrick and every other monger I asked fingered Humboldt Fog as the cheese that best captured the essence of the West Coast.

"Have you had Humboldt Fog?" they'd ask.

After a day, I had. It tastes salty, like the sea. In fact, it crashes on your palate as though it were a big, salty wave. Kaboom! Your palate is suddenly on its ass. Then the wave withdraws, leaving you stunned, your mouth soaked with brine.

What's odd is that, despite the salt, it feels luscious. The rind crisps against the *pâte*, and the thin, gooey layer laves through the whole as you chew. Its texture wowed me as much as its appearance and it helped me refine my idea of cheese-as-story: The beauties of Humboldt Fog showed me that a cheese starts telling its story even before it hits your mouth. You see a cheese, you squeeze and sniff a cheese, then you taste a cheese. That's how a cheese begins, before it middles and ends in even more tastes.

Curiously, in the story of Humboldt Fog, I neither saw, felt, nor tasted much fog, maybe because there hadn't been any fog in San Francisco since I'd been there. I remarked on this absence to Damion.

"It's foggy," he said, lopping a spoonful of plum, rosemary, and port jam that his wife had made onto the cheese, "and not only in good ways."

Stealing the spoon, I further remarked that Humboldt Fog struck me as a one-note cheese, pasteurized and rather empty once you got past its gorgeous looks and luscious feel. And as I covered its one salty note with jam, I mused that, perhaps, this surface appeal, this pretty-feely vacuity, might be the essence of the West Coast. I gestured, hazily, in the direction of L.A.

"Sure," piqued Damion, more into the jam than my musing, "if you mean it's not incredibly deep and tortured by history."

I finally experienced the San Fran effect. The fog brought it on.

One morning, after waking before dawn, I took the ferryboat across the bay to Sausalito. The fog was so thick I couldn't see the bridge or the city. Instead, I bounced on the gray-green swells and looked from the prow into the foggy veil that always seemed to draw back as the boat approached. The sun was rising, but through the fog it looked unnatural, like a moon lit from within and on the wrong horizon. Boat horns sounded, near and far, and, once, a huge cormorant flew by. I felt surprisingly calm, almost Zen. Chill, I believe. I didn't expect to see anything but fog and didn't mind.

And then the fog broke, or the boat broke from it, I'm not sure which, and I saw Alcatraz, raw and rocky on the stark bay water.

"Alcatraz," I said to no one.

The island was half-gripped by fog. It curled around the jagged coast and latched onto the rooftops. White and billowy, it made the island look—at least on the foggy half—like a cheese.

In an instant, I knew that the whole fog-bound city must look like this, like a giant bumpy cheese that rose out of the Pacific, stretched over the peninsula, and enfolded the Mission, the Marina, the Haight, and Telegraph Hill within its massive bloomy rind. I nodded slowly as the boat headed back into the fog and Alcatraz disappeared.

Yeah, I thought, I should move here.

The Hurricane
and the Vacherin

*M*ost tastings are tragic.
Wine tastings, cheese tastings, I've even been to a rhubarb tasting, but for all the carefully sliced samples, polished stemware, and fleshy participants, tragedy looms over the scene, as if Poe's raven perched above us, croaking, "Bon appétit!" We may be eating the Cheshires of merrie olde England or sipping the heartiest Barolos of northern Italy, but we're less merrie than muttery and rarely do we clink glasses, except as an unhearty afterthought. Said rightly, "*Cin cin*" can sound downright sad.

I'm overstating things. Still, tastings do often have a Poe-like pallor about them, one which isn't merely the result of throwing strangers together around a sweating Robiola. I suspect the reason lies in the nature of tragedy itself, because whatever else tragedy is, it's isolation—the lone soul cut off from the social body, Hamlet clad in solemn black, a blind Oedipus stranded in his own darkness. In tragedy, you're all alone. And, at most tastings, so is the food. You try your Pecorinos or your flight of Rieslings, each taste as ordered as test tubes or tissue samples, each offering up its isolated flavor. Sure, you compare them. You swish and chew your way to their relative merits, but that further isolates them. You note the fattiness of this Ginepro and that Pienza Stagionata di Fossa and, as you do, you make distinctions, divisions, and drive each cheese to its own lonesome end on your palate.

Tragedy has an aftertaste. It lingers insidiously on the tongue and works on you the way Iago's words work on Othello. It taints your once peaceful mind and shakes your once steadfast faith until one night you find yourself twisted up in your sheets, staring at the shadows on the ceiling and questioning what you hold most dear. Is gourmandizing, you wonder, all that great? Is cheese, you fear, all that great? And what about God? Does God exist, you ask in a dark-night-of-the-soul non sequitur, or is the cosmos just a cold, black void in which we all die cold and alone?

Taste enough tragedy and you start to search for God in a chunk of cheese.

In scale, the storm felt Old Testament.

After ravaging the Dominican Republic, Haiti, and Cuba, Hurricane Noel had at last hit Cambridge and, though no longer lethal, shook the branches above us with 50-mph gusts and pocked the streets with ceaseless rain. The leaves it had blown down had become a slick pulp on the sidewalk. Chuck and I were trying to keep ourselves and, more importantly, our cheese, upright.

"I don't slip on purpose!"

Chuck was in a cloche hat and wool coat buttoned to the collar. Earlier, when we'd first set out, she had embodied autumn with her red hair and rust scarf, but at the moment, she was a dark shade of storm. Her arms were clamped around mine because her feet kept slipping. She was worried we'd fall, and I had suggested that perhaps she was only pretending to slip because she didn't like how Hurricane Noel was getting all the attention.

"Besides," she continued, as I strained to hold her up, "I'm not that fat."

Uh oh. I knew if I showed any effort the next time Chuck slipped and clawed at my arm to prevent herself from falling, any effort—as I supported her, as I carried our cheese, as I steadied our umbrella—she'd think I was calling her fat. I didn't dare gasp or grunt. I didn't dare observe that the brim on her hat kept her from seeing where she stepped.

"Fat?" I said instead. "You're not fat."

This struck me as a good response, but I could sense Chuck cogitating. (I hadn't given the preferred response: "Fat? Are you mad? You're thin! So very thin!") So, I quickly changed the subject.

"Your hat looks great."

Chuck stopped and looked up at me. "It does, doesn't it?" Her eyes were bright.

"You look like Zelda."

"More like Katharine Hepburn."

"Much more like Katharine Hepburn."

There was Chuck, upturned lips, rain-wet cheeks, tendrils of hair sticking to her skin, and there was the world, alive with wind and water, and what did I do? Instead of leaning in for that unspeakably romantic kiss, I jerked back as the wind snapped our umbrella inside out.

"Maybe we made a mistake," Chuck sighed, glancing at

the plastic sack dripping from my other hand. "Maybe the cheese isn't worth it."

"Maybe," I said.

We gave up on the umbrella and stuffed it into a nearby trash bin, where it stirred like a mad tulip, and arm in arm we lurched toward home.

The cheese was worth it.

The cheese was a Vacherin and it came in a wooden box the size of a teapot. We smelled it the instant we shut the door. A whiff of grass and hay rose around us as we peeled off our layers. I decided to make a fire, Chuck went after a towel, and by the time she was fluffed and the fire was lit, our studio smelled like a field.

"Or a wet cow," Chuck sniffed.

We were sitting on the floor, the box between us.

"I'm going to open it," I said, not entirely sure I would.

We'd wanted to taste this cheese since we'd starting tasting cheese. We'd read about Vacherin in Paris, where Chuck had made the mistake of asking for it out of season. ("That, mademoiselle," the *fromager* had spat, "is a winter cheese," and Chuck felt a shopful of wintry Parisian stares.) Along with learning that Vacherin is seasonal, we learned that it's made in the villages of the Jura, a region just north of the French Alps, and that it's aged from three weeks to a month, which means it's illegal to import unpasteurized into the United States. That should have meant we'd have to go back to France to taste it, but a few months later, we got lucky. We heard where we could score an illegal Vacherin, and that's what had sent us into the hurricane. No violent rain or crashing branches were going to prevent us from tasting a cheese singled out and celebrated by a nation that, as Charles de Gaulle observed, has at least 246 cheeses. (Some counts go as high as 500.) Vacherin Mont d'Or was its full name, a cheese from the Mountain of Gold, and the mountain had come to us.

"Go on," whispered Chuck. "Lift the lid."

I lifted it. I lifted it and felt the air fill with the scents and stirrings of another world. On the Mountain of Gold, a clean wind blows across the rocks and bends the stiff, metallic grass. On the Mountain of Gold, wildflowers spot the slopes. On the Mountain of Gold, time stills. Late winter and early summer happen at once, and you sense the dormant earth rustling to life and hear the new calves bleat. On the Mountain of Gold, you look past the dilapidated barn and see in the distance the path your herd will take into the snow-capped heights. On the Mountain of Gold, you long to be nowhere else, because you belong here, you've always belonged here.

I was impressed. Inside its box, the Vacherin looked insignificant. It was pure white at arm's length, as though covered in eiderdown, and when you bent over it, you saw its gray dimples and butterscotch underbelly. But its smell was magical. Suddenly, I understood those tales about genies in bottles and keys to fairy kingdoms. I understood Pandora's box. And as I watched Chuck nosing it ("I almost feel it fizzing on my face"), I understood how something so large as my love for her might fit into something so small as a heart or how a soul might fit into a body.

The cheese, it seemed, was making a case for God.

*   *   *

I'm not the first to spy divinity in coagulated milk.

"Cheese does most gloriously reflect the multitudinous effect of earthly things, which could not be multitudinous did not they proceed from one mind." When Hilaire Belloc, one of the more eminent men of letters in Edwardian England, looked at cheese, he saw an argument not just for God, but Roman Catholicism:

> You can quote six cheeses perhaps which the public power of Christendom has founded outside the limits of its ancient Empire—but not more than six. I will quote you 253 between the Ebro and the Grampians, between Brindisi and the Irish Channel.
>
>   I do not write vainly. It is a profound thing.

Since cheese flourishes where the Holy Roman Empire once thrived, Belloc concludes that God—giver of cheese and all good things—must be Catholic. Belloc was famous for his faith as well as his titanic character (H. G. Wells once said, "Debating Mr. Belloc is like arguing with a hailstorm"), yet you can see from his protesting that he feels a little vain, a little cheesy, about arguing for the profundity of cheese.

Not so with his fellow Catholic, Mother Noella Marcellino. Known to her public as the "cheese nun," a name which irks her, Mother Marcellino lives in the Abbey of Regina Laudis, a Benedictine cloister in Bethlehem, Connecticut, where she and her community not only make a version of

Saint-Nectaire, but also where she studies *Geotrichum candidum*, a mold which grows on her own and other cheeses, such as Camembert and Reblochon, and helps give them their inimitable flavors.

"St. Benedict had a vision just before he died," said Mother Marcellino for a *New Yorker* interview, "in which he saw the world in a ray of light. For me, that's what it's like to see through a microscope. You look at the rind of a cheese and there's a whole world there."

I'm happy to report that the Catholic Church has not burned Mother Marcellino for her views on cheese. The Italian miller named Menocchio wasn't so lucky. In 1584, he faced the Inquisition for spouting—apparently to anyone who would listen—his theology, which he illustrated with cheese. He told his inquisitors:

> I have said that, in my opinion, all was chaos, that is, earth, air, water, and fire were mixed together; and out of that bulk a mass formed—just as cheese is made out of milk— and worms appeared in it, and these were the angels. The most holy majesty decreed that these should be God and the angels, and among that number of angels there was also God, he too having been created out of that mass at the same time . . .

In the beginning, there was milk, and out of this milk amassed cheese, and out of that cheese emerged worms, and one of those worms was God. It's an odd analogy. The inquisitors didn't get it either (who is "the most holy majesty" if *not* God?), but they didn't like it, and after more reports of Menocchio's heretical views and a second interrogation fifteen years later, they sent him to the stake.

Maybe Menocchio would have found comfort in knowing that earlier sages also used cheese to understand God and creation. The dejected Job, surrounded by his comforters, asks of his creator, "Hast thou not poured me as milk, and curdled me like cheese?" And that pagan Aristotle likened conception to cheesemaking. He thought that semen "acts in the same way as rennet acts upon milk," that it contains a "curdling principle." For Aristotle, semen causes a "coagulation" of blood in a woman's womb, and those curdles eventually form a fetal "cheese." To this day, Aristotle's fourth-century analogy lives on in the villages of the Basque country, where men make a rugged mountain cheese as they drive their flocks through the Pyrénées and newly pregnant women are met with a joyous shout: "You have been curdled!"

Zoroaster, Virgil, Hildegard of Bingen, the great gastronome Brillat-Savarin, all of them, perhaps even the Buddha, fathomed what G. K. Chesterton called "the holy act of eating cheese."

Cheese is cheesy, but it is a profound thing.

And we had yet to eat the Vacherin.

I tentatively jabbed at it with a kitchen knife (you have to cut off the top to get at the cheese), and it felt firm but membranous, the way a lung might if you pushed on it with your finger. I inhaled, Chuck exhaled, and I cut in. Outside, the wind shrieked. With small sawing motions, I worked the blade around the band of spruce bark that encircled it. The top, sticky and flapping, came off like a milky scalp. We peered into the Vacherin's innards. The *pâte* was the color of freshly churned butter and had a sheen that caught the firelight.

"I can still smell barn," said Chuck, eyelids aflutter, "but the shit's gone."

The shit was gone. The Vacherin smelled clean, green, how a cow should smell but doesn't. Chuck plunked a spoon into the viscous *pâte* and pulled up a gob. We argued for a moment about who should go first ("You." "No, you." "No, no, really, you.") and then, together, tasted it.

Simultaneous orgasm comes to mind, of course, but that's too easy. So does the Kantian take on aesthetic experience, in which Kant claims that only through art can you be sure other human beings have an interior life that resembles your own, because how can anyone else not feel as you do when you stand upon an Alpine peak and cast your eyes over Mont Blanc or when you shudder beneath the ceiling of the Sistine Chapel and succumb to the *terribilità*, the overpowering grandeur, of Michelangelo's masterpiece, as Raphael was reported to do when he looked up, saw Creation, and fainted? But Kant's too categorical. Chuck offered up her experience of reading *Heidi* at nine, but that didn't do it for us either.

"You almost feel coked out on it after the fact," said Chuck, who's never tried coke, but we agreed that the cheese was too earthy and unpretentious to be compared to a narcotic. Its taste escaped our metaphors.

As soon as it touches your tongue, the Vacherin diffuses,

creamy and clean, as much glass as grass, in a flavor so encompassing it pulls a note of metal from the spoon. Then it moves to a sharp tang, a buttery richness that owns your mouth and claims anything else in the air—the fire smoke, the cool rivulets of storm and rain that blew through the cracks in our shoddy windows. Until, at its end, it returns to the grass. It leaves you where you began, basking in a field on the Mountain of Gold.

As Chuck repeatedly dunked the spoon, I tried to describe the way it united so many flavors (and who knew hurricane had a flavor?) into one.

"The cheese," Chuck finally said, saving me from my gastronomical fumblings, "gives you the experience of what it's like to grow old with it. You can sit with it in a room for hours and not talk, because you both already know."

If most tastings are tragic, the best of them are comic. Not comic in the sense of a knee-slap or clown horn, but comic in the sense of celebrating community. So, instead of Phèdre in agony, you have the fairies, misfits, and lovers who romp together through *A Midsummer Night's Dream*, and, instead of Ajax's suicide, you have the weddings of Gwendolen and Jack, Cecily and Algy, just as soon as those dandies learn the importance of being Earnest. The best tastings don't separate tastes and cause tragedy; they join them and create comedy.

"Pairing" is the word experts use, but it's a bit stiff. Edward Behr, founder of *The Art of Eating*, notes as much in his review of the laboriously titled *What to Drink with What You Eat: The Definitive Guide to Pairing Food with Wine, Beer,*

Spirits, Coffee, Tea—Even Water—Based on Expert Advice from America's Best Sommeliers. Of pairing, he says, "the subject begins to be taken too seriously, if you consider that the main point of a drink, after all, is to provide refreshment." And Max McCalman warns us in *The Cheese Plate* that pairing, for all its seriousness, remains "an inexact calculus. Anyone who says otherwise is not telling the truth."

I believe McCalman is telling the truth, which is why I prefer comedy to calculus. Comedy is forgiving, drawn more to joy than calculation. And because comedy unites us, usually in laughs, sometimes in love, and maybe even in the way Dante believed all souls will unite at the end of that great journey he called the *Commedia.* In comedy, we become a little more than we'd be by ourselves. Dante and Beatrice, Don Quixote and Sancho Panza, Abbot and Costello, each can't exist without the other. What's a poet without a muse, a knight without a squire? And a straight man without a fat sidekick in a bowler hat? Well, he's just sad.

In the best tastings, as in comedy, things unite, like the flavors of grass, cream, rock, and breeze, like me and Chuck, like the hurricane and the Vacherin.

Little Chute, Wisconsin

*O*n a rainy Sunday morning in Little Chute, Wisconsin, after finishing a Big Cheese Breakfast of black coffee, orange juice, sausage links, pancakes, and a heap of cheesy eggs spiked with ham and green peppers, all served to us by the HOV Senior Service Club as part of the 21st Annual Great Wisconsin Cheese Festival, I bought a dozen chocolate-chip cookies.

There was no way Chuck and I would eat them. After three days of Wisconsin-sized portions, in which piles of macaroni salad precede sirloin dinners, and 24-ounce sirloins come topped with a stick of butter and buttressed with a twice-baked potato, we'd never eat again.

In the three days we'd been in Little Chute, we'd put down one actual meal. The rest of the time, we'd picked and snacked, though if you haven't been to northeast Wisconsin, you should know that a snack can mean a half-pound of provolone and an arm's length of beef stick. The senior with the silver ringlets who heaped my plate with sausages looked surprised when Chuck passed on the links.

Finally, I fathomed bulimia. And I could see Chuck was craving a smoke, despite the early hour and the cold rain, anything to help with the sixty thousand calories we'd just ingested.

"Careful there," said an old timer as we walked by the bake sale on our way out, "or you'll end up looking like me." He slapped his belly and smiled.

That's when we bought the cookies. In a few hours, we'd fly out of Green Bay, and though I'd been trying, I had yet to figure out Wisconsin cheese and I had pretty much given up. Why did so many cheese lovers I met *ooh* and *ah* over it? "Have you been to Wisconsin?" they'd cry. "Have you tried Wisconsin Cheddar?"

I handed my two dollars to one of the women working the sale, a gesture of good will, and asked, "What makes Wisconsin cheese so great?"

You might think that two days at a Wisconsin cheese festival would be enough time to figure out Wisconsin cheese. You'd be wrong.

When Chuck and I first strolled through the festival grounds at Doyle Park, we saw vendors selling funnel cake, hot dogs, and jambalaya. We saw dollar-a-ticket carnival rides, including an Octopus, a Round Up, a Rock-O-Plane, and an old-fashioned carousel. We saw the beer tent that sold Bud, Bud Light, and Bud Lime. We saw and rode Carlo the mechanical bull. (Chuck lasted twenty-eight seconds, compared to my twenty-three.) But we saw only one booth devoted to cheese. In a corner of the food tent, you could buy a one-pound bag of fresh cheese "curds."

I'd heard about these, a distinctly Wisconsin treat, one that supposedly squeaked as you ate it. I expected to see real curds, the white velvety kind shown in glossy books on cheesemaking. These weren't those. These were amorphous chunks of orangish Cheddar, about the size and shape of an orangutan's thumb. They were moist. They left an opaque sweat on the inside of the bag.

"Curds," I'd discover, are the building blocks of Wisconsin Cheddar. They get squished into much of the roughly 2.5 billion pounds of cheese that the state makes each year. Wisconsin produces a quarter of America's cheese, more than any other state, and the bulk of that is Cheddar and mozzarella. For Cheddar, the "curds" are crushed into giant, three-hundred-plus-pound blocks and aged for different lengths of time, sometimes up to eleven years, before the blocks are cut and packaged into shopper friendly sizes. "Curds" need quotation marks because they come into being a little later in the cheesemaking process than the word might suggest: After the real curds have been cut and separated from the whey, they're matted together into a giant layer; that layer then gets mechanically cut into bits; these bits are salted, as a typical cheese would be, and sold as "curds." As best as I can tell, Wisconsin cheese "curds" are essentially little cheeses used to make big cheeses.

"Do you want to try one?" Chuck asked.

A few samples sat out on a paper plate and, in the humid air, looked less than appetizing.

I suggested we wait. I was excited to taste one and

wanted to try the "curds" at their best. Munching down a tired sample in the middle of a crowded tent didn't feel right. Besides, I figured we'd enjoy them more after we'd watched the first official cheese event of the festival: the Celebrity Cheese Curd Eating Contest.

We got a Bud and made our way to the main stage.

For celebrities about to force-feed themselves a half-pound of "curds" on local television, the contestants looked in high spirits.

On stage sat Jan Hietpas from the BLC Community Bank, State Representative Al Ott, Action 2 News Anchorman Bill Jartz, Village Trustee Don Van Deurzen ("I've just had two big fajitas before this," he told the emcee when asked about his hopes for a win), and finally Al Zierler, the Cheese Festival Board President.

"All the celebrities have one-syllable names," observed Chuck.

It was true, and there were two Als. Little Chute seemed the sort of town where you don't need polysyllables, where you could do a lot with a "Hey, Al!" and a friendly nod.

Jan, Al, Bill, Don, and Al would each have to eat a bag of cheese "curds" as fast as possible, first person to finish wins. The emcee counted down, "Three, two, one, open!" The celebrities ripped into their "curds" and dumped them onto their plates in lopsided piles. And the "curds" flew.

Immediately, Bill pulled ahead. Television handsome, he has the rugged build of a linebacker and, we saw, the ability to eat like one. Yet he scooped up and deposited his "curds" almost daintily, as if he were nibbling finger sandwiches or truffles. He chased his "curds" with manly slugs of soda that showed he might have downed a Bud or two in his time.

"He's double-fisting it!" cried one of the highly madeup high-schoolers who stood next to us.

Bill was. Back and forth, hand after hand, Bill ate. Another "curd," then another, his squarish head swiveling atop his thick neck, pausing only to tilt more carbonation on the cheesy mass filling his round, handsome cheeks.

Al number one, who had finished second in last year's contest, could see he was outmatched. Waggishly, he slid a handful of his uneaten "curds" onto Bill's plate. But Bill ate on, unperturbed, in the zone. Then Fajita Don joined in the fun, throwing some of his own "curds" Bill's way. But on Bill ate, on and on, with as much of an anchorman's grin as he could muster for the camera that now zeroed in on his certain victory. He finished in two minutes and fifty-three seconds, setting his soda can down with a definitive twank.

We clapped and cheered, hooted and woo-wooed. Why, I'm still not sure. Perhaps because we loved a winner, perhaps because we admired a sport, but probably because we knew those "curds" Bill had just downed must have and would hurt. In the spirit of community, he had taken the hit for us all.

Only the high-schoolers, full of a healthy disgust for adult goofiness, held back. "That," ughed one, "is the most disgusting thing I've ever seen."

Chuck had wooed as loud as anyone.

She gets swept up in expressions of support: The choked-back tears of a widowed father as he watches his Olympian son bow for the bronze medal, the beams of a politician's wife as her husband accepts the nomination, not for himself, but for all of us, and any ovation that follows a lifetime-achievement award—Chuck thrills at these. The next morning, near the finish line of the Cheddar Chase Walk/Run, Chuck would woo again for the walkers/runners who crossed it.

The contest had her hyped. "We should try the 'curds' now," she said, "and see what they've just gone through."

We bought a bag and found a half-empty table where we could focus. Curds, we noticed on ripping into the plastic, have a painfully acrid smell. They're also clammy, like spoiled mushrooms. We each pinched one out of the bag and bit into it simultaneously. Then we chewed. And chewed. In silence.

"They're horrible," Chuck finally said.

"I taste whey," I offered, trying to stay neutral, "and a vegetal note."

"Oh," Chuck wheezed, "I can't eat another one."

We still had fifteen ounces of "curds" in the bag in front of us.

"At least they squeak," I said. I felt I should affirm something about them, and the "curd" did make endearing eeps as I chewed it. I couldn't, however, tell if the eeps came from the "curd" or from some sort of damage it was doing to my tooth enamel.

"Yeah," agreed Chuck, "in a pencil-top-eraser way."

We both took a long, medicinal pull on the Bud, then stared at the "curds."

"I can't throw them away," I whispered, "not here."

Chuck looked around, without trying to look like she

was looking around. She has the firm and erroneous belief that she would make a good undercover agent, which in everyday terms means she feels the need to punch me in the shoulder during particularly intense moments of *24*. Chuck's spy vision revealed the challenge we faced in Operation Curd Dump: There were several trash barrels, but all of them were conspicuous.

"You could carry them around," she concluded.

"All night?"

The Vic Ferrari Symphonic Rock Ensemble was already warming up on the main stage ("Check . . . check . . ."), and I didn't want to be the dork in the crowd holding the bag full of "curd."

"Just until it gets dark," Chuck said, *sotto voce*, checking over her shoulder for enemy operatives.

Dark was an hour off. I weighed my options: risk offending the Wisconsinites whose cheese we'd come to try by tossing out one of Wisconsin's signature cheese snacks at the very start of the Great Wisconsin Cheese Festival or tote around an almost-pound of inedible "curds" that would grow more warm and malodorous as the minutes passed?

Later, when the Vic Ferrari Symphonic Rock Ensemble launched into a cover of "Margaritaville," I surreptitiously dumped my "curds" and clapped along with everyone else.

Chuck and I shook off the "curds" and soldiered on.

A chilly rain pelted us the next afternoon as we weaved past the chainsaw-art demonstration and the petting zoo to attend the free cheese tasting. The line was long. We stood behind grandparents pushing strollers, middle-aged women hunched under umbrellas, and gangly kids in cleats. The tasting was taking place in a picnic shelter, and the tasters who emerged from it carried hand-sized paper plates heaped with cheese. The trick was to handle your umbrella and hold your plate, without dropping either. A few orange cubes tumbled into the wet grass, but no one said, "Shit!" Most times, the lost cheese just triggered a sweet, cheesy grin that showed up everywhere at the festival.

When Chuck and I reached the shelter, we worked our way down a long stretch of samples piled on aluminum trays and refilled by volunteers. Following the crowd, we piled our plates with provolone and string cheese, asiago and Cheddar, parmesan and mozzarella, Colby and pepper jack, brick cheese and Gouda, assorted cheese spreads, and an herb-flecked specialty called Uncle Charlie's Chicken Soup.

According to the state's Milk Marketing Board, Wisconsin makes more than 500 varieties of cheese, and we'd snagged a bunch of them, but, as we sampled, the "curds" struck me more and more as the extreme instance of the core flavors that rang through the cheeses. Sure, we could taste the variations—the parmesan had a dry smack, the pepper jack had a northern idea of south-of-the-border heat, and, in our Wisconsin cheese low, Uncle Charlie's Chicken Soup had a spice mix that brought back our childhood sickbeds—but still, almost all the cheeses trumpeted two notes above any other: salt and fat.

I shared this observation with Chuck, who observed, in turn, that salt and fat were essential foods, "evolutionary imperatives," that we were probably hardwired to find tasty so we could survive. I nodded, Chuck nodded, and we chewed on, thoughtfully.

Before long, we hit our Wisconsin cheese high: a native original called brick cheese, because it comes in brick-shaped packages. Brick cheese is a close cousin to Limburger. It has a sweet pungency that lingers in your mouth and sinuses, even in the rainy air, and its bite, while it has those same salty and fatty notes, transforms them into a pleasant tang that sits happily in the mouth.

"To make brick cheese," says Joe Widmer, whose cheese we were tasting and who was interviewed in *Cheese: The Making of a Wisconsin Tradition*, "we dip the cheese into whey every day for two weeks, then wrap it in foil. After three weeks it smells. You can't make a good stinky cheese, though, unless you start out with the best milk."

This was a good stinky cheese and, as Joe tells it, a favorite among Germans, who like to pair it with beer. "But sometimes," he explains, "wives won't let their husbands have brick cheese because it smells up the refrigerator."

I was glad Chuck was Irish.

"I don't know, but it is great!" exclaimed the tummy-slapping old timer.

To my surprise, the other seniors at the bake sale suddenly chimed in: "We've won lots of awards!" "We've got really good cheese here!" "We don't have all that waxy stuff like in Illinois!"

I nodded. Except for a lack of wax, the secret that made Wisconsin cheese great remained elusive, even to the seniors.

Yet, they obviously loved it. They spoke with such enthusiasm and earnestness, I couldn't but nod. I also couldn't miss the collective "we" that bubbled up in their answers. ("We've won . . ." "We've got . . ." "We don't . . .") The cheese didn't belong only to the cheesemakers. It belonged to the community, and for them its greatness was a given.

Chocolate-chip cookies in hand, I realized that Chuck and I had focused too narrowly. We'd been fixated, as we always were, on the cheese's unique properties. How was it made? How did it work in the mouth? And in our fixation, we'd overlooked the extent to which Wisconsin cheese gathered a community around it. The Celebrity Curd Eating Contest, the Cheddar Chase Walk/Run, the Big Cheese Parade, and Big Cheese Breakfast, they weren't really about cheese. That was why there was so little cheese at the Great Wisconsin Cheese Festival. And that, I'd say, is the greatness of Wisconsin cheese: Cheese was the occasion to celebrate Little Chute and, for three days in Doyle Park, cheese brought together a lot more than "curds."

The Whiteness in the Whey

The whole round sea was one huge cheese,
and those sharks the maggots in it.

—Herman Melville, *Moby-Dick; or The Whale*

*W*here did cheese come from?
Did some prehistoric goatherd think it up one lucky morning as he drove his flock along the bank of the Euphrates? Did a god bestow it on us, the way Meso-Americans once believed that Quetzalcoatl, the plumed serpent, gave us the cacao beans from which we make chocolate? Or did cheese just poof onto the *homo sapiens* scene like fire or the wheel? In Piedmont, there's a cheese called Robiola di Capra Incavolata that comes wrapped in cabbage leaves. Maybe cheese and babies share the same mythic patch.

Consider this: For milk to become cheese, it needs to curdle. I'll explain how this happens a little later, but for now just focus on the fact that the agent which causes curdling traditionally comes from enzymes found in the lining of a cow's, goat's, or sheep's stomach.

So how, I ask, how did an animal's milk ever mix with enzymes from inside that same animal's stomach in the first place? One story goes that animal stomachs were used to make storage pouches. So, maybe eight thousand years ago, someone tried to save their milk by pouring it into a stomach pouch that still had enzymes in its lining and, after a day of travel in which the milk and enzymes bounced around, that someone poured out curd.

Yet even that story doesn't necessarily lead to cheese. The fool or genius who looked at that clotted, rotted curd from that faulty stomach thermos still had to say, "Hey, I'm gonna mash this glop together and eat it!"

Although a food, cheese seems more like a colossal mistake.

Chuck and I wanted to make this mistake for ourselves. What does cheesemaking look like, up close and elbow deep in curd?

To find out, we went to Peter Dixon, the cheese fixer.

We'd first heard about Peter from one of our favorite mongers, Robert Aguilera. Robert had given us a taste of Peter's tomme, a ten-pound wheel dubbed Pawlet, after the town in which it's made, and it won us with a sharp zing that fades into a creamy sigh. It left our palate light enough to want seconds, then thirds. Robert spoke of Peter with hushed awe: Here was a cheesemaker with an intuitive sense of milk; here was the consultant other cheesemakers brought in when they couldn't figure out a problem with their cheese or when they wanted to make a new cheese or a new cheese cave. If a case involved cheese, Peter could crack it, whatever it was.

In the months that followed, we heard more whispers

from other mongers and cheesemakers, and soon I was cyber-stalking Peter.

He was off to Wayne County, Ohio, where he'd advise an Amish family on the construction of a cheese cave that would be cooled by ice cut from a nearby pond. He was in Winter Park, Florida, helping some citrus farmers turn the milk from their Jersey cows into a cheese named Bleu Sunshine. He was back from Seattle's annual cheese festival, where he'd given a workshop on *affinage*. And, all along, he was orchestrating the Farmstead Cheese Risk Reduction and Monitoring Program, a pilot project in which twenty-four New England farmers were "testing samples of milk, cheese, and the creamy environ-ment" to improve the safety and quality of farmstead cheese.

When Chuck and I finally made it to one of Peter's work-shops in southwestern Vermont, at a goat farm called Con-sider Bardwell, where Peter is the head cheesemaker, Peter had just returned from consulting with a fine foods company in Shanghai. He'd helped them develop recipes for Brie and other cheeses meant for cruise ships that docked in cheese-poor China.

"They got cows there," said Peter, smiling and scratching his spotty beard, "you'd be surprised."

Tall, lanky, and sweetly awkward, Peter looks like Shaggy from *Scooby-Doo*. He'd be laconic if his few words weren't so full of enthusiasm. He obviously loves acid levels and bac-teria counts, air flow and black mucor. And he gets jazzed when the process goes wrong—the milk doesn't heat quickly enough, a strange yellow mold shows up on a rind—because then he gets to solve a problem. If Peter had grown up with a chemistry set, he'd be missing his thumbs.

At one point in the workshop, I asked him why he wanted us to stir the curds so vigorously.

"Well, think about it," he said, unintentionally stressing I hadn't. "If the curds are full of liquid and they hit—" He brought his fists together six inches from my nose to illustrate smashing curds. As they hit, he opened his fingers to show liquid releasing from the curd so the curd could firm up.

Lesson over, he grinned at me from between his hands. What else was there to say? It was obvious. And cool.

Curd *is* cool, especially when it's cut.

Imagine a milky white surface, as round as an old well and shimmering. It looks wet, like you could plunk a stone into it and watch the ripples, but it's impossibly still. It makes the air above it seem animate. If you touch it, you might think of jello or the fleshy skin inside your cheek. It gives and it recovers, and although you'd expect its brilliance to throw your reflection back at you, it doesn't. When you stare at it, it swallows your sight in unvarying white.

You aren't the first person spellbound by such whiteness. It haunts Ishmael when he sails with Captain Ahab to hunt the white whale in *Moby-Dick*. Ishmael wants to understand white's power:

> Is it, that as an essence, whiteness is not so much a color as the visible absence of color, and at the same time the concrete of all colors; is it for these reasons that there is such a dumb blankness, full of meaning, in a wide landscape

of snows—a colorless, all-color of atheism from which we shrink?

That paradox, "a colorless, all-color," could describe the curd. It appears complete and empty at once, the mind of a Zen master approaching death. It draws you to it.

"Yet calm, enticing calm, oh, whale!" says Ishmael. "Thou glidest on, to all who for the first time eye thee . . ." Like Moby-Dick, curd has a whiteness that almost hypnotizes you.

Which is why it's cool when you cut it.

You run steel blades the length of your arm through the placid surface of the curd, slicing it into a perfect geometry. Long rectangles become shorter squares, and those squares, cut again, become triangles. Soon, however, the pleasing Euclidean shapes give way. The curd gets lumpy and irregular, piling on itself and dispersing in the sea of whey on which it floats. It bobs for a time until, cut to bits, it swims through the whey like plankton on the stiff currents your knives create. In the end, the blades are useless. The curd has become an uncountable number of milky flecks floating in a vat of whey the color of your teeth.

You could liken the pleasure of cutting curd to kicking down a sandcastle or cracking the caramelized sugar on a *crème brûlée*. As you slice up its uniform surface, you feel a little delight in destruction. Its perfect whiteness gets mangled, broken up, made as imperfect as the rest of us. Who hasn't wanted to stick a hand in freshly poured concrete?

But destruction isn't what's cool about it. What's cool is starting with that impossible stillness and stirring it. It enfolds, it erupts. It endures the sort of violence that must have marked creation.

When physicists pinpoint that moment just before the Big Bang, they may find—as Menocchio believed—curd.

Before cutting the curd comes lugging the milk.

Peter had swung by Jersey Girls Farm and picked up a bunch of large steel jugs filled with cow's milk. They were heavy, eighty pounds of heavy. As I helped Peter yank them from the truck bed and carry them toward the cheesemaking room, I noticed that my fellow workshop goers, eager at first, didn't return. (Chuck didn't even get up.) And by the time I got to the last jug, worrying that I now knew what a hernia felt like, Peter had also disappeared. I couldn't blame him. Not every step in cheesemaking drips glamour. It's sweaty work.

Exacting, too. The next step required us to pool the milk into a high-tech vat that could heat it evenly and stir it automatically. The milk had to climb to about ninety degrees, which, with 120 gallons, takes time.

Peter used that time to wax about "starters" such as "EZAL MA 400.1" and "TA050," bacterial cultures that get added to the milk soon after it begins warming and help shape the flavor of the cheese. The bacteria eat up the milk sugars and turn them into lactic acid, and that acid changes the overall acidity level in the milk, so that when the milk reaches the right temperature, its proteins can come together and form curd.

Curdling, however, doesn't start in earnest until the milk hits the right temperature and gets dosed again, this time with those liquid enzymes that traditionally come from the lining of an animal's stomach. The liquid is called "rennet" and, once it's mixed into the milk, it causes the milk's fat globules and proteins to clump together on the surface of the vat or "flocculate." It takes several minutes for milk to flocculate into curd, but once it does, the curd forms a solid white mass on the surface of the vat. The curd layer is held together by calcium phosphate, the same mineral in tooth enamel, and after another half hour or so, it's ready to cut into curds.

If that sounds complex, as though it involves test tubes and charts, it does. At least it does for Peter, who tests and retests acidity, measures milk temperatures, and merrily shouts out variables and variations that might come up in making this and other kinds of cheese.

"That's why I still do this," Peter smiled. "Every day, every week, it's just fun. I'll go to my grave and I'll be learning from the batch of cheese I just made."

That sounds true not only about Peter, but also about cheesemaking: There seems a lifetime's worth to learn. I absorbed as much as I could, but before long, I zoned out.

I wasn't the only one. I could see other eyes empty as Peter veered into the life cycle of bacteriophage or half-explained a pH electrode. ("I stopped listening yesterday," Chuck confessed when I asked her what pH was.) The only ones who fully followed Peter were his fellow cheesemakers, Margot and Leslie, two fresh-faced blondes who seemed better suited to Daytona Beach than a cheese room. I kept expecting them to crack gum.

Until, that is, I watched them take us through every step of the cheesemaking process and answer any question I asked (pH is the acidity level). Leslie and Margot run the farm's day-to-day operation, from cheesemaking to cheese aging. They also gracefully handle Peter's slips into the absentminded professor.

"That's the pump, Peter!" Leslie shouted over a churring sound that had just filled the room, "not the light!"

Holding freshly cut curd feels elemental, an experiment in water and air.

The curd has no heft, only a tingle of softness, like you've lathed your hand in the warm breath under Salome's veils. And yet it's wet. It goes limp and silky in your palm as the whey drips from it, and for a moment you're not sure if you're holding liquid air or airy liquid. You fight the urge to smear it on your face.

"After having my hands in it for only a few minutes, my fingers felt like eels, and began, as it were, to serpentine and spiralize." Ishmael is talking about a vat of spermaceti that's been harvested from the head of a whale, but he gives a good description of what it's like to swish your hands in a vat of curd and feel the whey break from it.

> As I bathed my hands among those soft, gentle globules of infiltrated tissues, woven almost within the hour; as they richly broke to my fingers, and discharged all their opulence, like fully ripe grapes their wine; as I snuffed up that uncontaminated aroma,—literally and truly, like the smell of spring violets; I declare to you, that for that time I lived as in a musky meadow . . . I felt divinely free from all illwill, or petulance, or malice, of any sort whatsoever.

When you snuff curds and whey, you smell butter and yogurt instead of violets, but you feel just as blithe. Your fingers squiggle and squirm through the vat effortlessly, and you live as in a bonnie dairy, among blonde milkmaids and ginger cows. You smile a lot.

Ishmael knew such bliss couldn't last.

"For now," he says, "I have perceived that in all cases man must eventually lower, or at least shift, his conceit of attainable felicity; not placing it anywhere in the intellect or the fancy; but in the wife, the bed, the table, the saddle, the fireside, the country."

You could add "the cheese," since, like Ishmael, you can't linger forever in freshly cut curd. You have to stir it so you can make it into cheese. And, as you stir it, as you whack out its whey, it becomes harder, lumpier, closer to rubber beads or boiled peas. Soon, it pills in your hands, ready for you to pour it into a cheese mold.

Still, like Ishmael, you remember that moment when you held together air and water and, when you do, you wonder if that felicity might not hint at another yet to come.

"In thoughts of the visions of the night," recalls Ishmael, "I saw long rows of angels in paradise, each with his hands in a jar of spermaceti."

Paradise might not include Leslie and Margot hooping curd, but they certainly could star in a 1940s number by Busby Berkeley.

The two stripped down to T-shirts and aprons so they could dunk their arms into the vat of whey and, with plastic pitchers, dip out the curd. At the same time, Peter opened a nozzle at the vat's bottom, and whey started gushing from it into a plastic tub. From there, a pump sucked it through a hose and ran it to a tank on Peter's truck. The whey would go to the pigs. The curd went into plastic hoops, cylindrical molds the same shape that the cheese would eventually take. The hoops have holes in them, so the whey can drain off, and as it did, it trickled down a long metal table and dripped into other plastic tubs in thin spotty streams.

The process happens fast: Leslie folding over the vat, dipping, hooping, the whey dripping; Margot folding over the vat, dipping, hooping, the whey dripping; sometimes in unison, sometimes alternating, sometimes pushing curd toward each other, sometimes shearing the vat's sides with strokes of their forearms, and all the while whey streaming from the table, splashing from the nozzle, and the pump churring in a turbulent, ebullient music. It looked choreographed, a dairy twist on the water ballet in *Footlight Parade*. When it ended, I wanted to clap.

"That's pretty much it," said Peter, after the hoops were full, and Leslie and Margot had pressed the curd firmly into them. "Now, they sit."

The curd had become cheese. Stark white cheese, cheese that needed aging, but definitely cheese. For the next few hours, the cheeses would be taken from the molds, flipped, and put back in the molds so the remaining whey would drain from them evenly. They'd also get stacked. The cheeses on top would press the lower cheeses, and each time they were turned, the order of the cheeses—top to bottom, bottom to top—would change. Tomorrow the cheese would get sunk in a salt brine so that the bacteria which were rapidly growing in it would slow down and it would start developing rinds, but Leslie and Margot would do that work without us. We were done. We'd seen what we wanted; we'd seen cheese come into being.

And we were a motley group. Not just Chuck and I, but also a retired Air Force officer who made cheese on the stove and aged it in a dorm fridge, an Amish farmer who wanted to make an Alpine-style tomme ("I've shod horses, and Cheddar is harder"), a commune dweller who was considering frozen yogurt in addition to cheese, an art dealer who never stopped checking his cell phone, a survivalist who slaughtered her own bulls and planned for the day when "the lines of supply are cut," and a seemingly meek mom in her mid-thirties who was about eight months pregnant and, in squeaky asides, gradually revealed that she was a native New Yorker, had five other kids, kept chickens, kept bees, kept cows, traveled throughout Maine helping other farmers set up and certify their dairies, and had decided to start making and selling cheese along with the yogurt, eggs, and honey that she already sold at the local farmer's market.

We were awkward conversationalists ("Say, how *do* you cut up a bull?"), so when Peter declared an end to the cheese-making, Chuck and I roamed off. We'd heard that in the barn up the hill the nanny goats had started giving birth and we wanted to see if we could see a kid.

We saw better.

"Was that water breaking?" I asked. As soon as we entered

the barn, I thought I'd seen a gooey outpouring from under a goat's tail.

"I don't know," said Chuck, whose eyes shuttled all over the path in search of spiderwebs and goat poo.

We swung around the pen for a closer look, and thirty or so Oberhasli checked us out. A species of goat originally from Switzerland, Oberhasli are a sandy chocolate brown with a black stripe that runs along their backs and black fur that cuffs above their hooves. They have alien eyes with horizontal pupils and dark irises, which make their stares coolly intelligent, as though they're judging you.

Sure enough, there was a nanny with two small legs sticking out of its rear. The nanny didn't seem to notice.

"I don't think it's supposed to come out that way," said Chuck, her face averted, presumably in case the water broke a second time.

"Should we tell someone?"

"I don't know, maybe."

The goat was less worried than we were. It munched hay and stepped around and, every so often, shivered in a way that might have been a contraction. It didn't look like it was trying very hard.

"It happens in the wild by itself, doesn't it?"

Neither of us really knew and neither of us wanted to cry, "Breech!" if the goat wasn't in any real trouble.

The goat shivered again. The legs poked out, then drew back in.

"I'll go ask a farmer," Chuck offered.

She hustled off, and I stood guard. For what, I don't know. I couldn't do anything except watch the goat. I wanted to grab the legs and yank out the kid—I felt up for it—but I had this feeling I'd break it. That tended to happen whenever I was around other people's children; I'd break them. I'd be sitting in a chair in someone's living room, and little Chelsea or David would scamper into the room and dive off the back of the couch onto an end table. The child would start yowling, and the parents would rush in and glower: "What did you do?!" I didn't want to break the goat. I vacillated. Should I yank, should I not yank?

Turned out that's what the farmer did, yanked. And as he yanked, the nanny goat screeched and yelped, and the kid and afterbirth slid from her in a rush of amniotic fluid.

Thump, the goat landed on the hay.

Chuck and I gasped.

The nanny goat went back to being bored.

The farmer picked up and scrubbed down the kid with an old towel. He set it, still slick and matted, by the nanny goat's udders.

The kid, all eight pounds of it, immediately collapsed on its spindly legs and immediately tried to get up, mahing the entire time. It might as well have been on ice, the way it buckled and fell. Mah, mah! But it was determined to get to an udder. Mah, mah! It heaved up again and again. It teetered, it tottered. Mah! And then it got there, and the mahing stopped, and the nanny goat licked it, and life in the barn went on.

"Rising with his utmost velocity from the furthest depths," says Ishmael, "the Sperm Whale thus booms his entire bulk into the pure element of air, and piling up a mountain of dazzling foam, shows his place to the distance of seven miles and more."

Where do these wonders come from?

I don't know. Maybe from nature, maybe from God or history or happenstance, a stomach lining and some milk somehow mix together and someone sees it, tries it, repeats it, and makes the first cheese.

I do know a wonder doesn't have to be a white whale and that even a newborn goat throws a mighty wake: One moment there's nothing, then there's a splash and a pair of twiggy legs and something that mahs and mahs and won't lie down. I know that water blends into air, air into water, and the old distinctions don't hold. Milk becomes chewable, a whale cleaves the heavens. Who can suss it?

Ishmael had it easier. For him, the sea was bottomless. No divers had scoured its floor, no submarines had shone a floodlight into its inky depths and watched the dragonfish and bristlemouths slide by. For him, there was a place from which a Moby-Dick could rise. He could point to the sea and say, "There, it came from down there."

Instead of the sea, we have science. Biology explains how goats are made. Chemistry explains how cheese is made. Cetology explains that when a whale breaches, it may be communicating with other whales or stunning nearby fish or oxygenating or cleaning the parasites from its skin. Science explains our wonder, and yet our wonder sticks around, even when we're smartened up, even when it shouldn't.

I wonder about that.

Stink

I don't want a sirloin steak,
   You can take pie and cake,
They give me a tummyache.
I like Stinky Cheese!

Liederkranz or Camembert,
   Soft Gruyere, Roquefort rare,
Gee it smells, but I don't care.
I like Stinky Cheese!

— "I Like Stinky Cheese,"
Dave Mann and Marty Fryberg

*I*n Ohio, where I'm from, we like stinky cheese.

Not stinky in the sense that Mann and Fryberg mean in their 1949 song, but stinky as in "poor quality," as in "I can't eat any more of this chipotle-pineapple cheese spread—it stinks." In Ohio, we like cheese spreads and cheese sauces. We like blocks of Cheddar flavored with Baco-Bits and cheeseballs encrusted with candied walnuts. We like squirt cheese, string cheese, Cheez Whiz, and blue cheese crumbles that come in precrumbled packages. In Ohio, we like Velveeta.

Being from Ohio, I didn't know cheese had a stinkiness

worth singing about until I left the heartland for the heartless East Coast. In New York, I discovered the nostril-quivering joy of Roquefort, the tearful power of an Époisses. In New York, I ♥ stinky cheese.

Indeed, stinky cheese helped me survive a New York that did not ♥ me. While a student at Columbia, I found myself in the bumptious job of catering receptions for famous poets (the first one I met sneered, "You're from Ohio? *Here* we pronounce that 'Idaho'"), and the stink of cheese saved my Ohioan soul.

Working reception meant you were setup and cleanup, the hands that wiped up spilled Merlot with a fistful of napkins and thrust crab puffs at doughy-eyed donors. You were infrastructure, invisible, nobody.

Not so to my Midwestern mind. To me, receptions meant red carpets and black ties, presidents and ambassadors, dinner mints. And to work reception! To greet the poets I'd come hoping to meet, to escort them from their lectures to their dinners to their readings to the receptions held in their honor—imagine me, thrusting a protective hand between them and the paparazzi—why, this was a thrill above all my hopes! How couldn't my aw-shucks modesty, coupled with my unmistakable brilliance, not end with invitations from the poets for Scotch, or sex, or Scotch *and* sex? I honed my postcoital pillow talk on Chaucer.

Ohioans learn slowly that their homespun anecdotes aren't appreciated by poets or that when a poet says, "Go away," he means it. I learned. Slowly. Slowly, I learned to shut up and work.

Yet, I did have one task I relished: buying cheese. For each poet, I was given a small amount of money to buy food—cheese, fruit, crackers, cookies—for the reception. Selecting wine was beyond my pay grade, but about twice a month I had forty bucks to spend at will. So, I'd walk the two blocks to Mama Joy's Deli and bother the guy in the worn apron who worked behind the counter. Back then, I knew little about cheese except that it came in colors, and my ignorance was surpassed only by my dogged optimism, which clearly grated this monger's nerves and grammar.

"What you want?"

"What's that?"

"You want smoked Gouda?"

"Is that what that is? Smoked Gouda?"

"You want that Gouda??"

"So that's Gouda?"

"Smoked Gouda."

"Good smoked Gouda?"

"It's Gouda. It's good."

"How good?"

"What how?"

"How do you know that Gouda's good?"

"How Gouda?"

"No," I corrected. For some no doubt bigoted reason, I decided he'd find it more helpful if I spoke to him in telegraphic bursts, which I tapped in the air before me. "I want—how know—how good—good Gouda."

"You wanting that Gouda or not wanting that Gouda!"

After my third trip to Mama Joy's, he started hiding from me.

How could he, how could anyone, understand that a good smoked Gouda was all I had to let the New York literati know I existed? I had no voice, no visibility. I had nothing—I was nothing—except a few cheese cubes stabbed through the heart with tinseled toothpicks.

How do you judge a poem?

You can judge it by its craftsmanship, as though it were a Ming vase or Amish chair. Does it hold together or fall apart? Does it work as it should? You can judge it in light of its zeitgeist, as though it were the Beatles' *White Album* or a hula-hoop. Does it typify its time? Does it evoke 1958 or 1968? You can judge it by its politics, its ambition, its philosophical or theological vision, its complexity, its use of rhyme or everyday speech, its subject matter, its ability to make you see the world anew or feel fuzzy. You can judge a poem by any of these measures.

You can also judge it with cheese.

Here's how: First, get a job as a cheese lackey for poets. Second, learn which poet you'll be serving and read that poet's work, savoring its quality. Next, go to your local cheese store and, with the help of your friendly cheesemonger ("You take that Gouda and you go!"), procure a cheese that suits the poet's work. Good poetry, good cheese. Bad poetry, bad cheese. Finally, at the reception, after the poet has finished reading, serve your cheese and watch the poet, along with everyone else, ingest your judgment of the poems. That's it.

Yes, you're right that when those luminaries and their

acolytes bite on an earthy Swiss Gruyère, they won't realize they're tasting the caseo-equivalent of the poet's subtle
iambic lines or that when they gnaw on a rubbery Cheddar,
they're re-experiencing the flavorless lyrics they've just heard
about ennui in the Baltimore burbs, but subliminally, while
they chit and chat, they'll link the poems that linger in their
ears with the cheese that fills their mouths. Subliminally,
they'll know what you think. They'll taste your taste.

So, though you may have to scoop up their olive pits and
fetch more Hefty bags, at least the cheese, indeed the cheese,
by God the cheese, will speak for you.

The cheese will say, "Your poetry is good."

The cheese will say, "Your poetry is bad."

And the cheese, when it's a rotting Roquefort that sweats
through the foil in which it's wrapped and reeks up the room,
will say, "Your poetry stinks."

Then again, with cheese, stink can lead to applause.

Go to stinkycheese.com and you're greeted with a sigh,
"Ah . . . the stink of cheese," as though Limburger had the
scent of a scrubbed baby. Go to the Artisanal Fromagerie,
Bistro & Wine Bar on Park Avenue and you can take a class
on stinky cheese:

> For most foods, stinky smells tell you to stay away!
> But not with cheese—in fact, the stronger the smell,
> the more delicious and delectable the flavor! Join
> Fromager Waldemar Albrecht as he demystifies the
> washed-rinds of stinky cheeses . . .

I haven't taken the class, but I have enjoyed the hurtful Morbier, with its gangrenous vein of blue-green ash, and I've survived a cheese from County Cork called Ardrahan that holds its own against whiskey. Between bites, I kept it on the window ledge. A cheese may smell like a sewer in August, but that doesn't mean it's not scrumptious. Poet Léon-Paul Fargue praised stinky cheese as "God's feet."

With poetry, stink isn't godly. For whether poets write about Achilles' grief or a lowly field mouse, they aspire to truth, to beauty, to knowledge, significance, or fame, but not to stink.

And yet poems about cheese—poems that celebrate what Clifton Fadiman described as "milk's leap toward immortality" —do stink. We have wonderful poems about other foods such as blackberries, oysters, and ale. We have immortal poems about wine. But, for cheese, we have stinky poems. Take the climax of an "Ode to Cheese," in which the poet asks God to bless the great cheeses of Europe:

> From hollow Holland, from the Voseges, from Brie,
> From Roquefort, Gorgonzola, and Italy!
> Bless them, good Lord! Bless Stilton's royal fare,
> Red Cheshire, and the tearful, cream Gruyère.

It stinks. And it's not alone. American cheese poems also stink, even when zealous Yankees such as Eugene Field hoist our flag against European curds:

> And cheese! No alien it, sir,
>   That's brought across the sea—

No Dutch antique, nor Switzer,
    Nor glutinous de Brie;
There's nothing I abhor so
    As mawments of this ilk—
Give me the harmless morceau
    That's made of true-blue milk!

Field may be true blue, but his poem stinks, unless he's brilliantly ironic in his use of the French "morceau" to defend America against the French.

And these are among the best cheese poems, poems that are bearable, even enjoyable in their stink. Most aren't. Most rhyme "cheese" and "please." Only a few have a stink that can rise, like Limburger, to immemorial heights. And only one stands as the stinkiest cheese poem—perhaps even the stinkiest poem—in the English language.

Hired hand, furniture maker, and coffin dealer, James McIntyre came from Scotland to Canada in 1841 at the age of fourteen. He eventually settled in Ingersoll, a small Ontario town in the center of Canada's dairy country.

The land seized McIntyre's imagination and his verse. He wrote poems about its history, its heroes, its authors, and its farmers. Its cheese inspired him most:

The ancient poets ne'er did dream
That Canada was land of cream,
They ne'er imagined it could flow
In this cold land of ice and snow,

Where everything did solid freeze,
They ne'er hoped or looked for cheese.

"The land of cream" so intoxicated McIntyre that he wrote about its dairy cows, its dairy men and maids, and its cheese-making, including how you should slop your cows, where you should house them, and when you should milk them:

Our muse it doth refuse to sing
Of cheese made in the early spring,
When cows give milk from spring fodder
You cannot make a good Cheddar.

The quality is often vile
Of cheese that is made in April,
Therefore we think for that reason
You should make later in the season.

Notice the "we." McIntyre spoke for his town, and his town embraced him. He read his poetry at dinner parties and teas, openings and socials, meetings of the Freemasons and the Odd Fellows. His was the collective voice that would, in his own words, "extol the fame of our town Ingersoll."

So, when, in 1866, Ingersoll combined its dairy resources and made a seven-thousand-pound mammoth cheese for an exhibition in Toronto—a cheese that would blazon to the world Ingersoll's cheesemaking power—McIntyre faced the greatest poetic challenge of his life. How would the town's great poet immortalize the town's greatest cheese?

I like to imagine him, circling the cheese, an unused pen

in his pocket, as he counts down the hours before the town gathers for its grand sendoff. A picture of the cheese from the Canadian Archives may capture this very event.

Were the town's expectations for McIntyre's poem as high as those hats? Was McIntyre's anxiety? I like to think so.

Yet, I suspect McIntyre finished the poem on the same night he heard the plan for the cheese. It has the feel of all his work, forced and eerily infelicitous. However he wrote it, "Ode on the Mammoth Cheese Weighing over 7,000 Pounds" achieves a stink almost unrivaled in English poetry:

> We have seen thee, queen of cheese,
> Lying quietly at your ease,
> Gently fanned by evening breeze,
> Thy fair form no flies dare seize.

All gaily dressed soon you'll go
To the great Provincial show,
To be admired by many a beau
In the city of Toronto.

Cows numerous as a swarm of bees,
Or as the leaves upon the trees,
It did require to make thee please
And stand unrivalled, queen of cheese.

May you not receive a scar as
We have heard that Mr. Harris
Intends to send you off as far as
The great world's show at Paris.

Of the youth beware of these,
For some of them might rudely squeeze
And bite your cheek, then songs or glees
We could not sing, oh! queen of cheese.

We'rt thou suspended from balloon,
You'd cast a shade even at noon,
Folks would think it was the moon
About to fall and crush them soon.

*   *   *

Impress, express.

That's one way we share our experience of food. Something edible—say, a seven-thousand-pound block of Canadian Cheddar—makes an impression on us, and from that impression we make an expression. We eat, we speak. If we're McIntyre, we write a stinky poem. His poem gives us a particularly ripe example of a common experience.

It also shows us a problem with thinking about food in this way, a problem we might miss if he didn't make it so noxiously noticeable. McIntyre, after all, expresses the mammoth impression made on him by the mammoth cheese. He recounts its epic creation. He praises its fair form. He predicts its noble destiny. He gives it a cosmic stature. He tries really hard. And he fails really badly. He doesn't immortalize the mammoth cheese as Omar Khayyám does wine or Dr. Seuss does green eggs and ham.

Why?

Is it because he hasn't any talent?

Is it because he hasn't actually tasted his muse?

Is it because he hasn't realized that the food which most affects us doesn't always result from an impression we express, but from a hidden part of ourselves that the food reveals, such that, when we taste it, we experience more of ourselves—we feel more rich, more complete—than we could if we hadn't tasted it and so, by eating it, become more fully ourselves?

I'm talking about Proust, of course. Even if you haven't made it through *À la recherche du temps perdu*, you probably know this part of the story: The narrator eats a madeleine with his tea, and its taste sparks memories of his childhood that he'd forgotten. "In that moment," he says:

> all the flowers in our garden and in M. Swann's park, and
> the water-lilies on the Vivonne and the good folk of the
> village and their little dwellings and the parish church and

the whole of Combray and its surroundings, taking shape
and solidity, sprang into being, town and gardens alike,
from my cup of tea.

For Proust, our memories are outside ourselves, locked away
from us. To free them, to experience once more those selves
we once were, we have to find the keys, and those keys are
hidden in the world around us, in a street's cobblestones, a
cup of tea, a madeleine. Proust reveals that we secret ourselves in the food we eat. In that charred hotdog is you when
you spent the summer in a mildewed tent. In that stale beer
is you when kisses were mysteries. In that tarragon, in that
beignet, in that Tabasco is you before you became someone
else because, in time, you are always becoming someone else
and leaving the selves you once were behind.

The foods that most affect us aren't always the seven-
thousand-pound cheeses that make grand impressions on us,
but those that give us back, if for a moment, our very being.
We eat and we are, again.

Sometimes, we call this comfort food.

"We want to go back to a time when life was not so complicated," says Marian Burros in *Cooking for Comfort*, "or,
at least, when we look at it from a distance, it was one that
seemed much simpler." Comfort food, Burros observes, fulfills
our desire for simplicity and safety, for the creamy, buttery
bliss of times gone by, even though we know that, in bygone
times, the world wasn't really so blissful. Comfort food feeds
our nostalgia.

Burros wrote her book because of a change she saw in the way New Yorkers were eating after September 11. Suddenly, rail-thin Manhattanites were sucking down plates of mac and cheese, and high-end diners who once frequented Le Cirque were seeking out that most familiar of chefs, Mom. "First our desire for comfort food was an effort to assure ourselves that the world had not come to an end," Burros explains, "even if the world as we knew it had. Now it's an assurance that everything is still, somehow, all right." Comfort food, Burros saw, can comfort us in the most uncomforting times.

That's true, but not the whole truth. September 11 merely makes vivid the fact that time itself isn't comforting. Every day, some world is coming to an end. Maybe it's the world of childhood or a home or a marriage, but when these worlds end, so do the selves who lived in them. We weren't the same after the towers collapsed, we know that, but we aren't the same each morning we wake. Though we don't notice it, the night steals from the self, which is why poets liken sleep to death and why the ticking clock unsettles us. The uncomfortable truth is that time always moves us in only one direction and toward only one end.

So, eating comfort food isn't just about going back to a simpler or safer time; it's about going back. The childhood mac and cheese whispers to us what the ghost whispers to Prince Hamlet and Jesus to his disciples: "Remember me." Remember who I was, remember that I was, remember all I've lost, remember who I've lost.

"It goes so fast," cries Emily at the end of *Our Town*, perhaps the most comforting play in American literature that doesn't burst into song. She's dead and she's just taken one last look at her life:

> We don't have time to look at one another. I didn't realize. So all that was going on and we never noticed. Take me back—up the hill—to my grave. But first: Wait! One more look. Good-bye, good-bye world. Good-bye, Grover's Corners. . . . Mama and Papa. Good-bye to clocks ticking . . . and Mama's sunflowers. And food and coffee. And new ironed dresses and hot baths . . . and sleeping and waking up. Oh, earth, you are too wonderful for anybody to realize you. Do any human beings ever realize life while they live it—every, every minute?

By taking us back, comfort food helps us endure the fact that, even before we die, we're dying every, every minute, and that stinks.

I don't know what the poets I gassed with Roquefort fumes remember when they whiff a stinky cheese, but when I whiff one, I remember a pluckier me. Today, eating a raunchy Taleggio makes me feel the same giddy joy I felt when I first set out for New York. Its stink preserves a self I'd hate to lose entirely.

And that goes not only for the stinky cheeses I buy in fancy cheese shops, but also for the stinky cheeses of Ohio. In my earliest memory, I'm in my room, wracked in the way only a four-year-old can be wracked. I've broken some rule or thrown some fit and been sent upstairs. I am sobbing. I am sobbing and looking at a Little Golden Book, and at some point, the door opens, and my parents enter. They are huge. They hand me a piece of plastic-wrapped American cheese, a Kraft Single. I unwrap the cheese and eat it in small, salty bites.

My parents must have said something—"Stop squirting the neighbor's dog with dish soap"—I don't remember what. I remember the cheese. The cheese said the only words a busted four-year-old needs to hear.

The cheese said, "It's all right. You're going to be all right."

Raw-Milk, Nonindustrial, Tradition-Rich Cheeses of the World, Unite!

*W*e call on all food-loving citizens of the world to respond now to the defense of the unpasteurized cheese tradition." This rallying call comes from the Slow Food "Manifesto in Defense of Raw Milk Cheese." It asks cheesemakers and cheese lovers to unite around "a food that has for hundreds of years inspired, given pleasure and provided sustenance but is now being insidiously undermined by the sterile hands of global hygiene controls."

Who knew cheese could spark a global revolution? Democracy, sure. Life, liberty, and the pursuit of happiness could understandably lead a group of tyrannized colonialists into a revolutionary war. And those early shots of Lenin rousing workers to break their capitalist chains, they hint at how the October Revolution shook the world. Even the Sexual Revolution makes sense. But cheese? *Formaggio a latte crudo*, wonderful as it is, doesn't seem the stuff of world-changing revolt.

Then again, neither does eating, yet Slow Food International—"a non-profit, ecogastronomic member-supported organization that was founded in 1989 to counteract fast food and fast life"—has managed to create a revolution that now includes over 100,000 members from over 130 countries, all fueled by a vision that starts at the table.

"Let us rediscover the flavors and savors of regional cooking and banish the degrading effects of *Fast Food*," wrote founding member Folco Portinar in the movement's first manifesto. It's an enticing idea: eating as uprising, lolling and loafing as sticking it to the system. And instead of asking you to dodge musket balls, storm factories, or free your love in a mucky puddle at Woodstock, this revolution asks you to partake in "suitable doses of guaranteed sensual pleasure and slow, long-lasting enjoyment."

Chuck and I signed up. This struck us as our revolution, especially if it meant eating raw-milk cheese. Before long, we were on the march to the medieval city of Bra, home of Slow Food, where every two years about 150,000 revolutionaries from around the world gather together under the Italian sun for the world's biggest celebration of *latte crudo*, a festival called "Cheese!"

"I keep thinking of zombie movies," said Chuck, making zombified eyes, "or those weird cartoons where everyone keeps jamming jamming jamming food into their mouths."

Entering the festival's International Cheese Market is not a slow experience, if by "slow" you mean "not frenetic." Thousands of eaters crush together beneath great white tents that trap the crowd's heat and mix it with the huff that rises from thousands of cheeses on display at hundreds of stalls. You find cheese from as far away as Tasmania and as near as the turret-topped hillsides you can see if you climb the city's thin, winding streets. You're jostled, squeezed, bounced about as you wait for a sample of Gran Guerriero, the "Great Warrior," an Italian sheep's cheese that comes in a thick nest of hay, which infuses its flavor and makes it look like a rustic ostrich egg. You're elbowed and *scusi*-ed as you check out the display of Marayn de Bartassac, who makes cheeses from France's Gascony and Guyenne regions that look nothing like cheese. They're small, brown, and gnarly, more reminiscent of mushrooms or ancient Egyptian fish carcasses than curd, and surprisingly beautiful. You pass Neal's Yard Dairy and gawk at the British Isles spread before you in cheese. You press on, to Switzerland, to Spain, to Germany and Greece.

And if the need for fresh air drives you from the tent, you're still in the throng, wedging your way among the booths that crowd the streets. Soon, you're trying a Kenyan yogurt that's made by farmers along the shores of the Terzoi and prepared with ash from the cromwo tree, which turns it a dreamy purplish gray and gives it an earthen savor. From there, you spot a massive sheepskin sack, round as a Louisiana watermelon and filled with lumpy crumbles of a Herzegovinian cheese called Sir Iz Mijeha ("cheese in sack"). The sack looks vaguely disgusting, and you start to feel gaspy, closed in and overwhelmed by the babel of languages swirling around you and the U.N. of curds crowding your tongue.

"Just the sight of everybody eating all day long," sighed Chuck, after we'd escaped down an alley, "knowing we're going to have to share a Porta Potti."

"Did you see those cheeses encrusted with grapes? Weren't those lovely?" I hoped to divert Chuck from thoughts of Porta Potties.

"How are those Porta Potties going to be after day five?"

"And that cheese made with wild thistle, that was delicious."

"I'd say about ninety-five percent of my experience is being filtered through the Porta Potties."

"I'm sorry," I said. Diversion wasn't going to happen, so I lit a cigarette, which Chuck likes to believe has fumigating, cleansing qualities, and handed it over.

A revolution, we realized, even a revolution based on pleasure, slowness, and raw milk, comes at a cost. Over the next five days, we would pay it in pee-length breath-holding, liquid hand-sanitizer, and getting grossed out as we watched our fellow revolutionaries paw the cheeses we were about to taste with hands that quite possibly, but not definitely, had been in a Porta Potti.

Inside the Great Hall of Cheese—not to be confused with the International Cheese Market, the Cheese Music Stage, Cheese Bimbi (for kids), the Wine Bank, the Birroteca, or the many booths at which you could get Sandwicheese—the pace became civilized, almost slow.

Under the tents, young volunteers in starched white shirts and black bow ties hustled back and forth with baskets of hearty bread and grissini, restocking small wooden tables where you could sit and breathe and taste the 138 cheeses featured in the Great Hall. The cheese waited in cases that ran the length of the tent, so you could see their shapes: a hulking disc of Comté from France, a spoonable skyr originally brought to Iceland by the Vikings, a Polish "oscypek" that comes from the Tatra mountains and has an ornate skin you want to stroke with your finger.

Curious, I poked around and saw that the American showing amounted to two cheeses. Pleasant Ridge Reserve from the Uplands Cheese Company sat next to Rogue River Blue from the Rogue Creamery in Central Point, Oregon. I felt a pang. No Vermont, no Maine, no New York or Massachusetts, and only two cheeses from the U.S. of A.? In numbers, that put us with Slovenia, Greece, and Bulgaria. In the eyes of Slow Food, it looked as though we were the Jamaican bobsledders of artisanal cheese.

I took hope from the fact that, as a country, we've barely begun making the sorts of cheeses that Slow Food celebrates. You might compare American cheese today to American wine during the late sixties and early seventies, when vintners in Napa, Santa Cruz, and Sonoma were figuring out how to make wines that would rival those bottled in the Old World. At the moment, the United States has around 400 to 450 artisanal creameries, according to Heather Paxton, an anthropologist at M.I.T. who studies American cheesemakers, but that's about twice the number from 2000. You can feel a surge, a momentum, an energy in the air like that greenish hum before lightning strikes. Okay, we may have only two cheeses representing us now, about thirty fewer than France and fifty fewer than Italy, but I figure it won't be long before our cheesemakers show the world America's caseo-kickassness.

Indeed, I later learned that all-American monger Anne Saxelby from Saxelby Cheesemongers was at that very moment back at the International Cheese Market, kicking ass. She was doling out tastes of Cowgirl Creamery Red Hawk,

Jasper Hill Bayley Hazen, and Michael Lee's Goat Tomme, all to the enthused *"Buonissimo!"* from cheese lovers who'd never had American cheese. Turns out that this year was the first time since the festival's start in 1997 that America has shown its cheese at Cheese!

We're just finding our place in the global revolution.

"Let's try the one that looks like a punching bag."

The size of a speed bag, Caciocavallo Podolico has a small horn at the top and a headlike shape that might very well make a boxer want to pummel it. Yet it also looks medieval, rusted, moldy on the rind, as though it's been hung in a dank cellar for a hundred years.

Chuck also referred to it as "the distended breast," a description that's less *crudo* than it sounds, since the cheese is made of raw milk and some of its horns have a nipple shape.

Slow Food has designated it a "Presidium," its term for cheeses and other foods it's trying to protect from extinction. ("Presidium," at its Latin root, means "protection," "defense," "assistance," and "aid.") Slow Food has over 300 Presidia, an endangered-foods list that includes Mananara Vanilla from Madagascar, Tuscan potato bread from Garfagnana, and Bario rice from the center of Borneo.

In the case of Caciocavallo Podolico, the threat involves the cows: The Podolica breed once ranged throughout Italy, but the cows don't give much milk. As a result, Italian herders have slowly replaced Podolica cows with more productive breeds; the cows now exist mostly in the poorer grazing lands of southern Italy, and if they vanish from there, the traditional cheese made from their milk and the local traditions of which it's a part may go with them. That's why Slow Food is working to promote the breed and the cheese. Slow Food has even intervened into Italy's agricultural policies, so that herders raising Podolica and other native breeds have a better economic climate in which to keep their cows.

With each of these Presidia, Slow Food tries to preserve a traditional food and, through it, a traditional way of life. Slow Food calls this undertaking its "Ark of Taste," conjuring up an image of 300 foods walking, two by two, up a gangplank to survive the storm of mechanizing, homogenizing, *terroir*-destroying, mass production.

Yet that image isn't quite right. Slow Food not only hopes to save traditions, it also wants to tout them as alternatives to a world that's being made into one big widget by industry. Not just survival, but revival—that's the revolution. Revolt against the production lines by returning to the artisans.

Revolt against exhausting the soil by returning to sustainable farming. Revolt against alienation, exploitation, and the rootless anonymity of fast-food life by returning to the local, the fair, and, above all, the flavorful.

"It tastes smoky," I said, "but with a growl." At first, I didn't find much about Caciocavallo Podolico that distinguished it from other smoked cheeses, except that it left a small angry grizzly bear in the back of my throat.

"Like Parmesan," clarified Chuck. She threw an inconspicuous jab into the air. "It makes me want to hit something."

I could see Chuck's point. The cheese was picking a fight with my palate, but after its initial punch, it began yielding less aggressive flavors. I could taste wildflowers, hewn grass, perhaps a vanilla pod. It took time, but the cheese slowly came alive in my mouth, showing me how its world worked and ours might: slow food, slow life.

What if it had tasted nasty?

Unlike Caciocavallo Podolico, some cheeses we tasted from the former Eastern Bloc did not make the best case for the revolution. After trying a few more Italian cheeses, Chuck and I assembled a tasting that began in Poland and ended near the Black Sea. By the time I had finished the final taste, a clammy Bulgarian sheep cheese made in the Balkan mountains, my tongue was coated with a stubborn effluvium that included pine needles, old rubber bands, a wool sock from a metal locker, and what I can describe only as a complete stranger's saliva.

Chuck didn't follow me on this Slavic journey. She saw

my reaction to the very first cheese and had the good sense not to start.

"You go ahead," she said, "but you don't have to eat them."

Ahead I went, because I have the regrettable need to eat whatever I take. I trace this need back to childhood, to what my parents called the Clean Plate Club, an apparently widespread and highly exclusive organization which they encouraged my brother and me to join on an almost daily basis and which was inspired, as I recall, by a starving child in China.

"He would love to have your beef stroganoff!" my mother would say, exhaustion in her voice, as my little brother pretended to vomit and I pushed around whitish meat clumps in the hope that displacing them would somehow make them look eaten. Eventually, however, the haunting specter of this unnamed, emaciated, stroganoff-deprived child ("He has *no* food") would guilt me into eating enough to see my plate, and then I was in, a member of the Clean Plate Club, and I could enjoy my brother's suffering.

In Bra, as the aftertaste of Slovenian and Romanian cheese punished me and not Chuck, it occurred to me that my mother's beef stroganoff was also a sort of slow food—my sixty-pound brother could hold out for hours—and that the Club itself was a sort of tradition, one I had never wholly shaken and one that, given what I'd just eaten, I probably should. In a pique of antirevolutionary spirit, I wondered whether some foods were even worth preserving. Besides, aren't revolutions usually about overthrowing tradition anyway?

I couldn't answer these questions about the Eastern Bloc

cheeses, but the nasty in my mouth did highlight a huge challenge that Slow Food must face: If you're building an Ark of
Taste, how do you choose what gets saved? And if your Ark
has only so much room, how do you choose what doesn't?

"I'm going to be something of a revolutionary."

Vittorio Beltrami had waited, silent and stony faced,
through an entire workshop that Chuck and I were attending
on pit cheese, a method of cheesemaking that developed in
central Italy's Emilia-Romagna region and dates back to at
least 1497. At last, Vittorio had the floor and he had a few
words of revolt, not against industrialized cheese, but against
his fellow artisans. He began by appealing directly to those of
us in the audience.

"I'm asking you to help us. Please help us."

Chuck and I were listening to him through headsets,
with the help of a translator whose English accent gave a
cool formality to his plea. Yet Vittorio moved us with his
grave look, two heavy eyes set between explosive tufts of
gray hair and a thick mustache. He wanted to explain why
he had broken with his fellow cheesemakers and the consortium that they had formed. The consortium is supposed
to unite the cheesemakers so that they can more easily protect, promote, and sell pit cheese, but in Vittorio's eyes, it
had become too big and, worse, taken on qualities found in
industrial cheesemaking. In other words, it had become too
much like the mass-producing monsters that it and organizations such as Slow Food are supposed to combat.

"We must know our animals one by one," Vittorio said.

"We must go back to the smell of cheese. We must return to the cheese shed."

Vittorio had made this return in his own career. He had started by aging and selling the cheese of other cheesemakers, but eventually began making cheese himself so that, as he later told us, he could understand the entire process. Now, he mourned the fact that the consortium had gotten pit cheese into supermarkets, where the customers were faceless, and could buy it at a price much lower than he felt it was really worth.

"It's an outrage," he went on. "This cheese must be expensive. To clean the pit," he said, stressing the work he has to do, "is something indescribable."

The pit or "fossa" is an aging cave that goes straight into the tuffaceous rock that marks the region. About three feet wide and nine feet deep, it has the shape of a flask. Its underground design originally allowed medieval cheesemakers to hide their cheese from thieves and papal tax collectors. Inside it, the cheese is bound in cloth and arranged along the walls. That done, the cheesemaker covers the pit with chalk or hay to absorb any moisture and create a seal. The cheese then ages for eighty to ninety days in what quickly becomes an oxygen-free environment, and this "asphyxiation," as one cheesemaker described it, means that the cheese will emerge from the pit tasting as though it's been aged for two or three years. That taste is powerful: Animal, sand, and urine attack your palate, and the end result is thrilling.

For us, Vittorio's cheese fared the best of the five we tasted, with flavors of vegetable surging from the rind and hay gathering in the center. But, because of this subtlety, a fellow pit cheesemaker accused him of not making a true pit cheese. Apparently, it should "destroy the taste buds." Vittorio replied that he loved his goats too much to obliterate the flavors in their milk.

The discussion got heated: Vittorio revolting in the midst of the Slow Food revolution, and the cheesemakers around him revolting against his revolt, and Vittorio never wavering in his belief that, despite the support of Slow Food and the success of the consortium—indeed, perhaps because of it—he heard "the death knell, the swan song" of pit cheese.

Vittorio's revolt suggests yet another challenge that confronts the Slow Food revolution: Once your revolution starts succeeding, how do you keep from reproducing the very system you've overthrown? How do you go from revolting against power to wielding it?

The term that Slow Food uses to list traditional foods, "presidium," reveals this danger. "Presidium" may have its linguistic roots in "save" and "assist," but a presidium is also a governing organization, one that possesses the power to lead and direct, such as the now-defunct Presidium of the Supreme Soviet of the U.S.S.R. or the Presidium of the Supreme People's Assembly that currently governs in North Korea. A presidium has the ability to protect, yes, but also the ability to control, and not always for the better.

As Chuck and I followed Vittorio back to the International Cheese Market, he alerted us to one possible way out of this danger: joy. For all his grim predictions, Vittorio exuded a joy for cheese and cheesemaking that shone as radiantly as his peach pants. We'd missed that joy listening to him in translation, but when we buttonholed him after the workshop, he was all enthusiasm, gallantly kissing Chuck's hand in a manner that "didn't feel at all fake or goofy." He spoke to us in voluble Italian, Chuck answered him in spotty French, I listened for English cognates, and none of us minded.

"Mio stand?!" he boomed, when we managed to convey that we wanted to see his other cheeses. Vittorio waved us after him and strode out of the workshop.

We could barely keep up. At roughly five feet and two inches, Vittorio moves like a cannonball, and though we could decipher only bits of what he said, he spoke joyously about his goats, his cheese, his family, and his employees, whom he also considers "famiglia." When we arrived at his stand, he began, all at once, conversing with us through his English-speaking daughter, joking with his fellow cheesemakers at the next stand, and welcoming each member of the crowd that had come to sample his jams, olive oil, and cheeses.

Watching him exhausted me. I began wondering how he could keep it up when he suddenly stopped and bellowed, "Gino!" into the air above the stand. Maybe he's mad? I thought. That would explain the energy he emitted. But then, from all over the massive tent, came shouts of "Gino!"

"There is no Gino," his daughter informed us. "Is a game."

We hung out awhile, enjoying the game and admiring the goat cheeses "tanned" with wild dill, with Montepulciano grapes, with anise, straw, and mint. The entire time we were there, Vittorio never stopped moving, double- and triple-checking everything, joking, laughing. His delight in the entire scene lit us and, we could see, the folks who stopped to try his cheese. When we eventually left, with a cheese, a "God bless you," and a big cheek-kiss for Chuck, we couldn't believe that an enterprise full of so much joy would go sour.

Perhaps in Vittorio's example, as his name suggests, lies victory.

Fortunately, Slow Food has kept joy at the core of its revolution.

You could see it in the charming design of the red snail on the water cups, in the bounty of 953 regional wines to pair with the cheeses, in the triumphant cracking of a seven-year-old wheel of Parmigiano-Reggiano made with milk from the rare white cow, in the master classes, demonstrations, children's activities, and traditional meals that took place every evening down the side streets of Bra and in the nearby countryside.

For me, the most joyous moment happened on the music stage, where local school kids put on a pageant dressed as giant pieces of cheese. ("Give me four years to teach the children," said Lenin, "and the seed I have sown will never be uprooted.") At its climax, they danced a musical number that was somewhere between a cheerleading routine and a hoedown. There was Fontina, swinging his arms with Pecorino Romano. There was Buffalo Mozzarella, wiggling her spirit fingers alongside Provolone and Gorgonzola. And there were all of us, in the crowd, cheering and clapping and singing along to "If I Had a Hammer," "Let's Twist Again," and "Mamma Mia," as the kids wheeled and two-stepped and grinned.

Slow Food might be growing into an international power, but from our spot in the crowd, it looked like what Slow Food had attained—by preserving traditional foods and bringing us together to celebrate and eat them at Cheese!—was the power to spread joy.

Long live the revolution!

Feeling Cheesy

*A*cross America, you can rent a multitiered cheese fountain to celebrate any occasion, "including," as Choco Fountain Inc.'s Web site explains, "wedding receptions, birthdays, dessert buffets, catered events, banquets, class reunions, family reunions, Bar Mitzvahs and more." Nacho or Cheddar cheese bubbles down the fountain's tiers in a thick yellow current. You catch it with a corn chip or other "dipping item":

> Cocktail Weiners, Meatballs, Bread Sticks, Assorted Breads, Pretzels, Chicken Wings, Taquitos, Chicken Tenders, Cheese Cubes, Potato Wedges, Cubed Smoked Ham, Sliced Sausage, Steak Cubes, Potato Chips, Baby Carrots, Cherry Tomatoes, Cauliflower, Broccoli Florets, Radishes, Celery Stalks, Pineapple, Red, Yellow, Orange & Green Pepper Strips, Etc.

The fountain comes with long skewers that reduce the risk of cheese splurting on your bridal gown or Steelers jersey. The mini, three-tiered model rents for $149.99 and includes access to a 24-hour support line.

If dipping cheese cubes into melted cheese doesn't entice you, you might consider donning a Cheesehead hat, a pair of cheese earrings, or a cheese necktie ("For the executive with everything"). Attired in cheese, you can groove to jazz musician Han Bennink improvising on drums made of real and fake cheese or watch performance artist Cosimo Cavallaro cover iconic supermodel Twiggy in spray cheese. You can also snuggle up with the business bestseller *Who Moved My Cheese?* and learn, through an allegory in which cheese stands for happiness and success, how you can handle change. ("The quicker you let go of old cheese, the sooner you can enjoy new cheese.") You might finish the book feeling so good that you point your camera at yourself and say, "Cheese!"

Cheesiness surrounds us, and if you consider all the cheesy things that have nothing to do with cheese—Hallmark cards, Harlequin covers, Kodak moments, a cappella groups, gold-dipped roses, any emotion fit for a musical—it can feel as though cheesiness engulfs us.

But what is *cheesy*? When we say, "That's so cheesy," what do we mean and why does cheese, yummy and innocent cheese, convey our meaning? What do we feel when we feel cheesy?

"Inferior, poor."

My *Webster's Pocket Dictionary* didn't help. Its definition of "cheesy" is inferior and poor, but not cheesy.

I needed more than a pocket's worth of dictionary power. I grabbed a hefty, Herculean tome and looked up "cheesy"

again: "Of poor quality; shoddy." That wasn't much better.
Another dictionary gave me "shabby" and "cheap," but not
"poor." The inconsistency surprised me. Curious, I checked
out about twenty more definitions from different dictionaries.
I wanted to see if the lexicographers agreed.

They did and they didn't, and as I tried to track their
slight differences on a scrap of paper, it occurred to me that
I could transform them into a digitized word cloud. You've
probably seen one: an image made of different words of different sizes. In this case, the size of each word in my cloud
would capture the number of times it was used by lexicographers to define "cheesy." The larger the word, the more
frequently it showed up in their definitions. The smaller, the
less frequently.

I made my cloud at a Web site called Wordle, which
is a great way to lose six or seven hours. You paste in text
from any source—the Constitution, the *New York Times*, old
e-mails—click "go," and out comes a word cloud. I dumped in
all the definitions, and here's what I got:

Those three titanic words leap out. For lexicographers, "cheesy" is "poorly and cheaply made." Its foremost meaning lies in worth and workmanship, "quality" in the sense of value. Only after that first big flash does cheesy's nature, its character and quali*ties*, emerge. Smaller words stress "cheesy" as chintzy, tacky, and clichéd. So for lexicographers, when you say, "That's so cheesy," you make a judgment first and give a description second.

That emphasis seemed off when I considered the cheese fountain. Made of stainless steel and given a 10 year life expectancy, it's apparently easy to operate, assemble, and clean, since all of its "food zone parts" are dishwasher safe. Its makers tout it as built to last and I don't doubt them. Why would a company that specializes in making fountains that circulate edible food (you can also use melted chocolate, eggnog, barbecue sauce, and ranch dressing) not make them well?

Yet the fountains, which include ATA-approved cases with telescoping handles and casters, are cheesy through and through.

Even the font that I used to make my word cloud troubled the dictionaries' emphasis. Grilled Cheese wasn't shoddy or cheap. It was, however, cheesy.

The lexicographers had gotten "cheesy" wrong or, if not wrong, not quite right.

A look in the *Oxford English Dictionary*, the 20-volume, 22,000-page granddaddy of all English dictionaries, told me why. The OED not only gives you definitions, it also gives you dates. You can learn what a word means and the first time it appeared in print conveying those meanings. In 1398, for example, John de Trevisa first used "cheesy" to mean "of or belonging to cheese; consisting of, or of the nature of, cheese; abounding in cheese." He included "cheesy" in his translation of a medieval encyclopedia called *On the Properties of Things* in a sentence about whey: "Wheye that is thynne and watry wyth chesy party synketh downe to the grounde." With that "chesy," Trevisa gave lexicographers the first instance they've found of "cheesy" in English.

"Cheesy" as a slang term shows up 500 years later. An 1896 entry in a book called *Student Slang* reads: "*Cheesy*, a vague term of depreciation." The OED cites it as the first instance of "cheesy" meaning "inferior, second-rate, cheap and nasty."

It takes almost fifty more years before "cheesy" starts to mean "tawdry, hackneyed, unsubtle, or excessively sentimental, especially if nevertheless appealing; 'tacky', 'kitschy', 'corny.'" It occurs in the screenplay for *Hail the Conquering Hero*, a 1943 comedy by Preston Sturges, and the way it's spelled and the context in which it appears hint at its meaning: "Of all the cheezy songs I ever heard . . . that one certainly takes the crackers." Cheese and crackers, cheesy songs. That's a familiar sort of "cheesy," the sort that describes cheese fountains, cheese hats, and cheese fonts. At long last, the "cheesy" of Hallmark had arrived on the American scene.

And Hallmark came up with the hallmark for cheesiness one year later. In 1944, at a meeting, on a cocktail napkin, a salesman scribbled down, "When you care enough to send the very best." The next year, Les Brown took Americans on

"A Sentimental Journey," Bing Crosby dreamed of a white Christmas, and Perry Como loved "Till the End of Time." In 1946, *The Yearling* and *It's a Wonderful Life* vied for the Oscar. And in 1947, Norman Rockwell began publishing his most popular calendar art, "The Four Seasons," and the four seasons lasted—through publication and republication—for seventeen years. Cheezy "cheesy" is an American original. Next to this meaning, the OED notes "orig. U.S."

So, maybe the reason lexicographers weren't getting "cheesy" right is that they were stuck in the past, preserving what "cheesy" used to mean, rather than capturing its present meaning? Their definitions retained the moldy whiff of 1896. Moreover, they were mired in the *English* language, when the latest meaning of "cheesy" was, like the cheese fountain that illustrated it, "MADE IN THE USA!!"

Clearly, I needed to ditch those dictionaries and get American. Hello Jersey! Hello Junction City and Sunset Strip! I needed to hit the mean streets and hear how today's slang talkers jibed with "cheesy."

Turns out "cheesy" has a few new meanings.

When you're cheesy or "cheesed," you might be stoned, as in "Man, old boy Fat Cheddar was cheesy as fuck after blazin' that Phillie Titan." You also might be flush, as in "My wallet is cheesy." You might be hungry, flabby, or hip. You might be using unfair or repetitive methods to win a video game or you might be "the grit that formulates in the hole of your fleshy when streatching your ear." You might also be "someone who is really stupid and rehabbed."

These definitions and examples come from the *Urban Dictionary*, a Web site that invites any user to contribute a definition for a slang term. As new terms and meanings are added to the site, the dictionary's users then vote—thumbs up, thumbs down—on the quality of those definitions.

As of February 2009, "cheesy" had twenty-five definitions and about 3500 voting thumbs. The ones I've just mentioned are among the least popular and most badly spelled. The big loser (49 thumbs down, none up) comes from a contributor named "AD-og," who defines cheesy as "The state of being lethargic or lazy. Can also be used to refer to something too difficult or involving excessive amounts of work." AD-og demonstrates:

1) Person 1: "Let's go get some tacos."
   Person 2: "I am way too cheesy. Let's just sit here."

2) Person 1: "We have to finish this school project, dude."
   Person 2: "Man, it is way too much cheese."

Although AD-og got creamed in the popular vote, I've included him and some of the other losers because their definitions show how words keep sprouting meanings. You never know when a new one, a "cheezy," for example, will take root and grow. Maybe in ten years, you'll collapse into a La-Z-Boy recliner and say with complete clarity, "I've cheesed too much cheese today to be anything but cheesy."

The losers also lend some legitimacy to the winners. If forty-nine thumbs turned down for AD-og's definition, and 762 turned up for redhen's (82 down) or 575 for eiricky's (154 down), then maybe this populist approach has merit. It certainly rings of the American ideal: Let the people, not the lexicographers, decide what "cheesy" means.

Heady with idealism, I took the more popular definitions and put them through the same process I'd used before. The text went into Wordle, and I waited for the word cloud to float up. Here is the people's "cheesy":

And here is the "cheesy" I know. Not the elite, antiquated, Anglocentric "cheesy" of lexicographers, but the sappy, campy, tacky, corny, kitschy, vulgar, lame, stupid, fake, overdone, cliché ridden, sentimental, all American "cheesy" that was totally and mysteriously, in the upper-right corner, "taco." For the people, description and judgment are one. Saying "cheesy" means defining quality, as in value, and qualities, as in nature or character, together. This "cheesy" was balanced. This "cheesy" made sense.

*   *   *

Satisfied as I was, I wasn't finished. Redhen, who has also defined "money," "pimp," and "fascistonista" ("merely a synonym for fashionista"), makes a point about cheesiness that calls into question cheesy's very character.

Cheesiness seems to belong to whatever strikes us as cheesy. The cheese fountain would be cheesy, we think, whether it burbled at the biggest Super Bowl party in Las Vegas or in the woods where a tree falls that no one hears. Cheesiness seems to exist independently of us. Say, "That's so cheesy!" and you're saying some thing, "that" thing, is cheesy. You've spotted cheesiness, out there, in the world, as though it were chicken pox or pebbles.

The lexicographers' definitions also suggest this view. Whether you go with cheesy as "poor" or cheesy as "taco," both definitions stress that cheesiness is objective, a quality of cheesy things. Just look at that '80s prom dress.

That's not redhen's view. For redhen, "Cheesiness is subjective." It involves a reaction to objective things, but a reaction that varies from person to person. As redhen explains, "What seems cheesy to me, may be a legitimate and attractive hairstyle to you. What seems cheesy to me, may cause you to weep and hug your girlfriend tight." The cheese fountain may, in some mind that I have trouble imagining, be "cool" or "fun," maybe even "elegant," but not "cheesy." In turn, I have to allow for the likelihood that what I find cool, fun, maybe even elegant—writing a book on cheese, say—may strike a mind who has trouble imagining mine as cheesy.

So, cheesiness works more the way beauty or bullshit does: You know it when you see it, but you can't be sure anyone else is seeing it with you, because what you see has to do with who you are. Your tastes, your standards, your ability to stomach a cheese cube lathered in hot nacho cheese, that shapes what you'll call "cheap" or "taco" and, consequently, "cheesy." When you say or don't say, "That's so cheesy," you're saying it less about "that" than you are about yourself.

Which is why the cheesiest things in the world are things other people find profound, heartfelt, and sincere. How many cards has Hallmark sold? How many parties has the cheese fountain perfected? How many tears has Jimmy Stewart jerked ("Hello, Bedford Falls! Merry Christmas, you wonderful old Building and Loan!") as he galumphs home to his wonderful life? The cheesiest things aren't meant to be cheesy; they're meant to move you and they do move others.

Yet, as those around you tear up or swell up, you're unmoved. You don't find the card touching, the fountain enticing, the acting convincing. You find them cheesy.

So, if cheesiness has to do with you, what happens when you find *yourself* feeling cheesy?

To investigate, I left Wordle and went to We Feel Fine, a Web site that records feelings. Every day, it scans the Web for new blog entries that use the phrases "I feel" and "I am feeling" and then archives them. Its database includes millions of sentences and adds fifteen to twenty thousand more each day. You can poke into data on almost three thousand five hundred feelings. By April 2009, it had recorded 736 occurrences of "cheesy," which lagged well behind "better" at 128,155, but ahead of "grotesque" at twenty. I read them all.

By far, the archetypical cheesy statement is "I feel cheesy." It has variations—I feel "so cheesy," "very cheesy," "incredibly" or "horribly cheesy"—but none of them reveal much about feeling cheesy except that it's often extreme and not entirely pleasant.

The more telling "cheesy" statement involves a "but." It starts archetypically, "I feel cheesy," but then butts on:

> i feel so cheesy saying typing things like this but: love is beautiful

> i feel somewhat cheesy paraphrasing the most hated line from american beauty but sometimes beauty overwhelms me

> i know i am getting a little bit cheesy right now but what the heck that [is] how i feel for you and it does not give me more pleasure and happiness than to tell you how much i care about you no matter how cheesy it may be

In an "I feel cheesy, but . . ." statement, feeling cheesy works as an acknowledgment and apology. When I feel cheesy, I feel cheesy because I'm feeling something else—happiness, love, heartbreak, elation—and I sense that this something else might be cheesy. Yet, rather than not feel this something else, I acknowledge and apologize for it ("I feel cheesy . . .") then go ahead ("but . . .") and feel it anyway.

Feeling cheesy isn't a feeling in itself. It's a feeling you have about another feeling, a feeling your internal cheese-ometer tells you is cheesy. When you say, "I feel cheesy," you're experiencing emotions that, if they weren't yours and even when they are yours, make you say, "That's so cheesy!"

So, why not reject them? If you're aware you're being cheesy, why not stop yourself? Unfortunately, cheesiness has an attraction akin to vampires and gravity. It can seem inevitable, compulsory.

> i feel so cheesy and sappy and mushy but i can't help myself

> i feel so cheesy lately but i can't help it

> i feel like this hugely cheesy sentimental sap but i can't help it if my eyes are misty and my hearts all over the place

You're sappy, a huge sentimental sap, and you know it. Yet you can't but succumb, can't but submit. Your cheesy feeling owns you. You're helpless.

That helplessness may arise because what you feel, though cheesy, is true.

As I read through hundreds of cheesy feelings, I kept noticing an "I feel cheesy, but it's true" statement that I found quite touching. Of course, feeling touched about blog posts made me feel cheesy, but as I read them, I saw people struggling to prove the truth of their own emotions against the charge of cheesiness. And since that charge comes from within, feeling cheesy in these instances amounted to reckoning with self-doubt. If I feel cheesy, can I believe what I'm feeling? And what if my feeling matters to me? What if I need it or need it to be true?

> i feel kinda cheesy trying to sound psychological and all but honestly its really how it is

> i mean i feel like im writing something cheesy that should be read aloud at the end of a movie while the font is being followed with a camera but its true man

> i feel like most of my life has been lived on the edge and i know it sounds kind of cheesy to say that but i can assure you it is the only words i can use to sum up what its been like

> i feel cheesy saying this but its true

Sometimes cheesy words are the only words you have, sometimes cheesy feelings are the only ones you feel, and sometimes that cheesiness might still be true.

Sometimes feeling cheesy is really how it is.

Most times, though, it isn't.

Most times feeling cheesy means pretty much what you'd expect it to mean: You feel a pang of inauthenticity, an itch of insincerity. You feel more fake than real, perhaps because these itches and pangs don't prevent you from feeling. Perhaps because you'd rather feel this emotion, however cheesy, than not feel at all.

"We all *want* to have certain feelings," writes D. H. Lawrence, "feelings of love, of passionate sex, of kindliness and so forth. Very few people really feel love, or sex passion, or kindliness, or anything else that goes all deep. So the mass just fake these feelings inside themselves. Faked feelings! The world is all gummy with them."

Lawrence might have said "cheesy," except that when you're feeling cheesy, you admit you're faking. You 'fess up. You say, "I feel cheesy" or "That's so cheesy!" and you know, even if no one else does, that what you feel or what you see is faked. You can thrill at the faux elegance of the cheese fountain and you can sport the faux *joie de vivre* of your cheese necktie because you know they're faux. You can read *Who Moved My Cheese?* and admire spray-cheese art because they're cheesy, of course they're cheesy, didn't you just say they're cheesy?

Cheesy feelings don't go all deep, but they remind us of our depth. Like rubber needles, they poke at our capacity and desire to feel. Cheesy feelings reveal, maybe even lance, our longing for true ones.

That's part of their pleasure. You might have spotted a few surprising terms in both the lexicographers' and people's definitions of "cheesy": "awesome," "cool," "happy," and as the OED puts it, "nevertheless appealing." That affirmation makes sense. Why can you buy hanging dice in the shape of large Cheddar blocks if cheesiness weren't, in some way and as Cheesehead.com cries, "FUN!"?

You might speculate that the dice arise from a collective self-hate, but it seems telling to me that cheesy things and cheesy emotions tend to be harmless. Hallmarks don't hurt,

not really, and even heartbreak, when it's cheesy, doesn't lead
to a handful of barbiturates and a fifth of Smirnoff. You're
more likely to stay in your pajamas, listen to "I Will Always
Love You" on repeat, and bake a pan full of brownies that
you eat alone or with a BFF who assures you that, yes, you'll
love again. You sniff and shake your head: No, never, never,
give me another brownie. You're not suffering, not really, so
much as indulging in suffering, faux suffering, and at no one's
expense. Neither you nor your BFF are worried about you, not
really, and there's little chance you'll show up at the door of
your ex at three in the morning with a butcher's knife and a
slaughtered rabbit.

So, cheesiness enables. It lets you enjoy emotions that
are mostly fake, yet nevertheless appealing. When you feel
cheesy, you believe in feelings, just not in the one you're
currently feeling.

What does any of this have to do with cheese?

Why has cheese come to signify all that's sappy, campy,
tacky, corny, kitschy, vulgar, lame, stupid, fake, overdone,
cliché ridden, and sentimental in American culture? What's
wrong with "corny" or "soupy"? Why did cheese have to be
sacrificed on the food-as-adjective altar? It's not fair.

The answer might lie not in what cheese is, but in what
cheese was. In 1943, the year Americans started saying
"cheesy," Word War II was on. Food was rationed, and the
cheese that people were eating wasn't artisanal and organic.
It was industry. It was Kraft. In 1943, you could trade one

rationing coupon for two boxes of Kraft Macaroni and Cheese Dinner, and Americans at home ate about 80 million boxes that included an orangey powder labeled "cheese."

American soldiers had it worse. The K-rations they ate for lunch contained biscuits, sugar, salt tablets, cigarettes, gum, and a "cheese product" that could patch holes in airplanes.

"Whatever they used to preserve the cheese gave it properties of remarkable toughness and rubbery resilience," recalls gunner Jim O'Keefe, in an interview for HistoryNet.com.

On December 7, 1944, O'Keefe was part of a bombing raid on Mukden, a city in Northeast China that was occupied by Japanese forces. On the flight out, O'Keefe's B-29 encountered Japanese fighters that shot through his plane's nose and destroyed his gun sight. The cabin started losing pressure. The plane turned back. O'Keefe and the crew began stuffing the bullet holes with rags, but there weren't enough. That's when Edwin Mann, one of O'Keefe's crewmen, spotted his lunch. He opened it and plugged up the remaining bullet holes with two packages of K-ration cheese product.

Cheese wasn't cheese as we now know it when Americans started saying "cheesy." It was a fake, a substitute, not only for meat but for metal. Is it any wonder that it became slang for other fakes, other substitutes? You might call cheesiness an "emotion product." The label on it says "happiness" or "love," but when you experience it, it feels powdery, rubbery, not quite real.

And yet, in a time of deprivation, it gets you by. Maybe not in the way its makers expect—laughing at cheesiness may be its most important function—and maybe in spite of it. I imagine the quality of cheese wasn't what mattered most to Rosie the Riveter when she got back from a factory shift and was able, in less than ten minutes, to gather her family around a hot meal of mac and cheese. And I imagine that's not what matters now to those of us who eat the more than one million boxes of mac and cheese that Kraft sells every day.

Perhaps that's why "cheesy" has a hint of affirmation. It might be fake, but it means well. If we had a choice, we wouldn't rid ourselves of it, even if it annoys us from time to time, even if "cheesy" is unfair to cheese.

While I was musing on cheesy, I made a call to my grandma.

She'd just turned ninety-one, and I wanted to wish her a happy birthday before she headed off to the American Legion in Waynesville, Ohio, where she registers voters and volunteers with elections, or to the nearby seniors home in Lebanon, where she helps take care of "old folks." She lived through the Great Depression and raised a family during the war while my granddad was stationed on Parris Island. She's the most loving person I know, though in a no-nonsense, let's-get-everybody-to-the-table-and-fed sort of way. There's little about Grandma Mary that's cheesy except her love of cheese.

"Right now, I've got two . . . no, three open cheeses," she said. Grandma Mary lives alone, and I could hear her rattling through the fridge, which is always stocked to serve twelve, "and of course a Colby-Jack."

I wondered what "cheesy" would mean for her. She was

born in 1918, grew up on a horse farm, and, as I soon learned, bought her cheese during the war from the butcher, who kept a large wheel of it in the back of the store.

"You'd say, 'Give me a hunk of cheese,' and he'd whoop it right off."

When I asked her about government cheese, she bristled. That was "for the indigent" and clearly not cheese she'd had in her kitchen or served to her family.

"How many people were you cooking for?" I asked. I still can't sort out all the names she mentions when she starts reminiscing.

"Oh, anybody who came by."

That's Grandma Mary. Stop by, and she feeds you. We talked about how she made macaroni and cheese back then (hand grated, "so the chunks didn't gum up"), about the string cheese she now has for breakfast every morning (with coffee and the puzzle), and her general take on cheese ("Cheese to me is just part of enjoying food"). I got around to asking her what "cheesy" meant.

"You mean like a cheesy idea?"

"Sure," I said. I didn't want to direct her answer more than I already had.

"That's a good idea," she said. "That means 'really put together.' A cheesy idea is one that's all held together."

Up the Mont, to the Fort

*O*n the Mountain of Gold, lynx with jagged fangs and a hunger for human flesh stalk you through the waist-deep snow, their howls carried by an icy wind that shreds your skin and claws your eyes. On the Mountain of Gold, you stumble and falter and can't see the ledge from which you'll fall, for over a mile, shrieking at the gray, heedless cliffs until you're impaled on the gnarled branches of a lightning-scorched pine. On the Mountain of Gold, the sun sets in an instant, and the air thins to poison. On the Mountain of Gold, you don't come down. Not, at least, if you're Chuck.

If you aren't Chuck, if you're, say, one of the dozens of happy skiers who whisked by Chuck and me as we trudged toward the peak of Mont d'Or on a pleasant, sunny afternoon in early February, you might find coming down the Mountain of Gold a pleasure. Although that afternoon, you might have wondered about those weirdos, that guy in the frayed scarf taking pictures and that woman in the vintage fox-fur coat and floppy-eared, Holden Caulfield cap, who didn't seem to know about snowdrifts or snowshoes.

You might also have wondered why she was crying or why, every so often, she flung herself melodramatically onto the snow, as if never to rise.

The answer lies in the chasm that can sometimes open between fantasy and reality. It was into that chasm that Chuck had fallen and, coincidentally, it was that chasm that had brought Chuck and me back to France, so we could climb, with a water bottle and a belly full of Vacherin, the Mountain of Gold.

Our fantasizing began back in Cambridge.

As we explored Formaggio, we found ourselves caught in a happy gravity. Every cheese that wowed us, wowed us in that soul-bliss sort of way, would turn out to have come from the same small region in France, the Jura. We'd try a sticky, stinky Morbier and see it was made in the Jura. We'd sample three wholly distinct, wholly delicious Comtés and see, on the labels, "Jura." We'd find an enticing tomme and see ("Hurrah!") Jura.

We got curious. We'd heard about Normandy, Burgundy, the Île-de-France, and the Côte d'Azur, where Picasso kicked around, but the Jura?

We looked for it on a map and saw a strip of mountains that ran alongside the Alps. Geneva was the closest city, and not too far off, though in the opposite direction, was Dijon. Google gave us more—some tourism Web sites, some photos of lush forests and snowy hills—but not much more. The bland facts we found on Wikipedia didn't explain why Jura cheese tasted so good.

And where facts failed, fantasy crept in.

We began inventing the world from which these cheeses came. "What's the Jura look like now?" we'd ask after a half pound of Comté and together we'd conjure up an answer. It usually involved windswept fields and rocky slopes, the lone bong of a cow bell.

We weren't entirely to blame. At Formaggio, the mongers fueled our Jura fantasies. One would tell us about an old stone fort, buried inside a mountain, dark and labyrinthine and filled with 65,000 wheels of the best Comté in the world. Another would tell us about Bleu de Gex or Cancoillote, sumptuous cheeses that never made it out of the Jura. Still another would mention the Forêt de la Joux, full of evergreens and enchantment.

The Jura became so unbearably magical for us, we decided

to go. We wanted to taste these cheeses in their world, not ours, and see if their taste changed. How would the Jurassic air inflect a Comté? How would scaling Mont d'Or flavor a Vacherin Mont d'Or? And Gex and Morbier were towns as well as cheeses, which meant we could eat Bleu de Gex in Gex, Morbier in Morbier.

To make the trip happen, we had to fantasize more about our finances than our destination, but we bought two pairs of snow boots and practiced wearing them in the slush puddles of Cambridge.

After all, how many chances do you get to adventure into a fantasy?

Eventually, we found ourselves thousands of feet in the air, off the coast of Iceland, flipping through *SkyMall* and playing What Would You Buy If You Had to Buy Something.

"The Bigfoot-Yeti Garden Statue," I started.

"The Deluxe Digital Massage Boots," Chuck countered.

"The Dough-Nu-Matic Doughnut Maker."

"The Three-Pac Ultrasonic Pest Repellent."

"The Branding Irons."

"The Traveling Pet Seat and Safety Harness."

"God, I hate flying," I blurted. My haunches ached, and the in-flight movie was so bad I loathed myself for watching it.

"*You* hate it?" Chuck's eyes widened in wonky circles. She hates flying with every Dramamine-saturated cell of her being and she'd been trying hard not to complain. Here I'd usurped her right to first bitch.

Deeply wronged, Chuck detailed the agonies of flight: single-serving meals of unknown origin, dehydration, deep vein thrombosis, ghastly smells of unknown origin, turbulence, terrorists, stewardesses, sitting too near the toilet, sitting too far from the toilet, coughers, snorers, chatterers, "and of course the pervasive impulse to vomit," Chuck added with a haughty head bob, "because of those bags."

I backed off. I'd been beaten.

It did, however, occur to me that Jurassic cheese, which makes the same trip that we were currently making, must undergo its own ordeal. Storage crates, shipping containers, refrigeration, customs delays, and no *affineur* fussing over it in the cargo haul or the truck bed. If we felt battered flying coach, how must a cheese feel after a 3,661-mile trip from the Jura to Cambridge? I was amazed it still tasted so amazing.

And how much better would it taste when, figuratively speaking, it hadn't lived on airplane coffee or tried to sleep on a foam pillow the size of a smurf's laundry bag? How much better if the cheese never had to cross mountain peaks, for the first time, in winter, with Chuck and Dramamine at the wheel, along cliffs studded with thick ice and boulders that could fall and crush your brittle Prius rental car, and where the roads keep turning, ninety degrees, 180 degrees, 270 degrees, before turning just as crazily in the opposite direction, and where the trucks barrel at you, directly it seems, and the horns behind you blare a decibel above your thudding heart, because you can't bring yourself to go over ten miles per hour, how much better would the cheese be then?

"I can't help it if they're upset," Chuck shouted a few

sleepless hours later, behind the wheel, as she watched the traffic stacking up in the Prius's rearview mirror.

"Ignore them," I said shakily.

"I can't go any faster!"

Chuck wrung the steering wheel and hit the gas. I felt my stomach slide into my right thigh as we went into another turn. If we ever made it to the Jura, we would need a soothing slice of cheese.

The French, unlike us, have made a collective choice not to make themselves miserable.

They take two-hour lunches with time to leaf through the paper or sip a café, instead of staying at the desk and dipping a Power Bar into a Red Bull. They work thirty-five-hour weeks, instead of sixteen hours over the weekend. They spend less time toting around their children and enjoy them more. They eat less and enjoy it more. They make love more and enjoy it more. And they spend up to eight weeks a year on vacation, sun glinting in their unlined eyes or off their well-waxed skis, while we use our vacation to have that colonoscopy we otherwise can't squeeze in. The French have turned their time into richer and fuller lives.

On the whole, I admire this attitude, even though my weekend usually starts on Saturday evening at sevenish and ends around midnight, with Chuck and me trying to finish flossing before fatigue drags us under. Still, the French sense of time, and time off, can make it difficult to do things in France, such as obtain a cheese.

We blew through Gex because we hadn't factored into

our planning the ten-mile-an-hour drive over the mountains, so not getting Bleu de Gex in Gex was our fault. And
later, when we rolled into Morbier in the early afternoon, we
couldn't find a *fromagerie* with an open door. At the *Fromagerie de Morbier*, we could see the mongers though the window,
right there, lunching and lounging. We could even see the
cheese, but our gaunt, desperate faces steaming up the glass
didn't draw from them so much as a glance.

They were right, of course. We were the barbarians, the
American ids demanding what we wanted when we wanted
it, which was now. So, not getting Morbier in Morbier
was also our fault, a fact that didn't prevent Chuck, soul
wrenched after the drive, from bursting into tears in the
parking lot.

That was it: too much reality.

Weeks before, when we'd planned the trip, we'd fanta-
sized about our first taste of the Jura being a cheese in the
Jurassic town for which it's named, but to do that we'd have
to wait an hour in a snow-encrusted parking lot, and that
wasn't worth it, not in our haggard state.

So, we junked the fantasy and ate lunch at a kitschy restaurant across the road that catered to a tourist's need for
now. Our food was fatty, overpriced, and presented with too
much flair, and our waiter held our check hostage for a cruel
hour, probably out of some need to teach us an unnecessary
lesson in French time. We left feeling fatty and abused, but
rested enough to go on.

Back in the Prius, while Chuck worked the brake at the
green light, we ignored the horns escalating behind us and
rallied our hopes for Poligny.

*   *   *

Poligny didn't disappoint.

It lies in a nook created by limestone cliffs that encompass it on two sides and looks cut from the forest and fields that surround it.

On the southern cliff, above its medieval streets and umber roof tiles, a large metal cross rises broodingly into gray sky. To me, it felt more of conquest than faith and conjured up an image of Roman soldiers marching on Gaul and staking out the horizon for Caesar. Historically, that's wrong, but the *Croix du Dan* invites legends. One is about grateful parents who built it after their love-stricken son refrained from riding his steed off the cliff and damning his soul. Another is about Anne of Brittany, who eyed the spot on her return from a pilgrimage to Saint Claude in 1499 to pray for a child. She ordered that a cross be built and, months later, gave birth to her only heir, Claude. If the cross can bear legends about near death and miraculous birth, why not one about empire?

Aesthetically, that's right. The cross is steely and sparse, made to endure, and the Romanesque buildings that sit under it evoke the town's early history. In Poligny, time seems to stretch from before the Gallic Wars up to the fifteenth-century Cathedral of Saint Hippolyte, and from there to the statue of Napoleon's general, Jean Pierre Travot, who served in the nineteenth-century revolution and whose swaggering figure now greens in the town's center, around which we circled in our twenty-first-century hybrid, looking for a place to park.

The best part of Poligny isn't the fusion of history and

legend or nature and culture that you sense in an idyllic town of five thousand people; it's that when you finally park and stand near General Travot, you see three cheese shops, all a few steps away.

Chuck and I entered Epicurea, a *caviste* and *crémier*, almost at random. Airy and bright, the shop has a modest, friendly vibe, with a cheese counter and a chummy bar running down one side. On the other side, large windows light the racks of local wines that angle inward, like the leaves of a large book, and beckon you to read their labels.

We had never seen, never knew, there were so many Jurassic wines to be drunk. In Cambridge, we could find a few, usually at too high a price, and here were hundreds. From around the bend, across the valley, the town next to the next town. For a moment, we forgot about cheese and asked the sprightly middle-aged *fromager* with the bright blue eyes for a recommendation. She pulled a Trousseau, with "animal" qualities, and she and Chuck fell into a chat. At some point, Chuck mentioned that we didn't have a wine opener and where could we buy a cheap one, since we couldn't take it back with us on the plane?

The *fromager*'s eyes clicked to her eyebrows, then she ducked behind the bar and came back with an old plastic opener that she plunked in our bag along with the Bleu de Gex and Comté she'd selected to go with the Trousseau. We *merci beaucoup*-ed her *beaucoup* times, but she just smiled and shrugged us off.

Poligny, it turns out, is that kind of place.

*   *   *

The Trousseau smelled of plowed earth.

"Is it corked?" Chuck asked, who asks this about any wine or cheese that has a stinky whiff.

It wasn't corked, but it did have flavors of bark and—sure enough—animal. It also behaved animal. It clawed at our palates, with tangy but not tannic nails, though its mouth-feel told you it had to have tannins. It tasted rustic, gruff, as though aged with hunks of withered vine inside the barrel. It couldn't have been more drinkable or better suited to the cheese, which we were eating underneath the thin covers, in three layers of thermal wear, jetlagged, at three o'clock in the morning.

Which is how we found out about a virtue of Jurassic cheese and wine: It fortifies you. And not in an American way. Here we look to food for defense. Cancer, age, and obesity threaten us, and cabbage rescues us with roughage, blueberries preserve us with antioxidants, and sugar- and fat-free oat muffins stuff us with zero calories. Food defends us, but for us, the enemy lies within. Our cells could turn on us, our genes could turn on us, our adipose tissue could turn us into tubs of human Crisco. We eat to defend ourselves against ourselves.

In the Jura, the enemy lies without. Cold gathers in the high pines and creeps down the slopes and through the walls. Darkness grows immense and runs its thin sinewy fingers along your bones. In the Jura, you and your body confront the same threats. Allies, you need a fort.

Fortunately, the Jurassians figured out how to fill this need eons ago, and with a bottle of wine and a pound of cheese, you can hold out through a cold, dark night. At first, the

Trousseau that you nurse chills you like well water, but then you warm to it, or it warms to you, and by the time you've finished half the bottle, it spreads directly from your stomach to your skin. You feel rosy, radiant, even if you're bruise blue. And soon, as you gnaw on Bleu de Gex and Comté, you're no longer feeding yourself but a small fire that smolders just behind your navel and pulses outward, enveloping you in a cozy bubble of cheesy warmth. After a few chomps of Jurassic cheese, you're cheery, defrosted, fortified.

And that doesn't mean you aren't also swooning.

The delicately flecked Bleu de Gex breathes out its scents of toffee and whisky, and, as it opens in your mouth, you taste an herbaceous tang, maybe a hint of nuts roasted on an old metal drum. It doesn't do anything you'd expect from a blue. No salty, moldy bite, no wince. Instead, it sighs away on your palate as you admire the hatched flecks that score its *pâte* in irregular shapes, leaving open swaths of cream like the mists that move through a Chinese painting. And the Comté—is that buttered popcorn? It can't be, and as you continue mush-ing it against your teeth, you decide it's nut, nut and caramel, nut and caramel and must, but good must, and who knew there was a good must? You shrug and take another bite or you slug the Trousseau, which you now see you're drinking from the bottle.

What happened to the cold? Who cares about the dark? You're fine. It occurs to you that if you lived in the Jura, you'd have to do this everyday. Comté every day! Trousseau every day! Bleu de Gex not once in a lifetime stuffed with cabbage, muffins, and medicinal blueberries, but every day! Agex and agex and agex!

*   *   *

"I've eaten Comté every day of my life," said Maurice Etiévant, drawing his index finger across the table in a sharp, definitive line that ran from his birth to that morning in the village of Mesnay.

Chuck and I had arrived at Maurice's farm an hour earlier, after passing it a few times.

"Did you see it?" Chuck would ask, swiveling the Prius too quickly into someone's gravel drive so she could make a K turn. The tires crunched as we craned our heads back toward the village. For me, farms were Midwestern monoliths. I spotted them from the air whenever I flew home to Ohio: silos, barns, a single house with a dirt drive that led straight from a road named "route," all surrounded by fields that went on, uninterrupted, until they reached the next farm miles and miles away.

Maurice's farm, when we finally rolled up to it, was wedged among the village houses. Next door, his neighbor's laundry slumped on the line. His rabbit hutch and the first Montbéliarde cow we spied, mud-bellied and massive, scratching its nose on a post, seemed oddly out of place, scrunched in. The old swing set across from it felt more to scale. Later, Maurice would tell us that some of the villagers get impatient in the early spring when he has to drive his herd back and forth along the roads to reach the pastures that surround Mesnay (after a winter in the barn, the cows' hooves are too delicate for them to stay up on the hillsides), and I could see how thirty-five Prius-sized cows could clog local traffic.

"We're making it for here," Maurice emphasized, his arms

spindling from his thin frame in a sharp, angular motion. His eyes fixed on his fingertip from behind his rough beard. "From here, for here," he said. "Its purpose is here."

Forty years ago, when Maurice started working the farm with his father, he saw the excitement that local cheesemakers felt about industrializing. Then, in such cases as Cantal and Camembert, he saw industry slowly ruin the cheese and traditions it once served. Profits rose, quality vanished, and in an export-driven, mass-produced "nightmare," the cheese lost "what was unique and precious," its *terroir* and its link to the people who made it.

"I make my cheese for locals," he said with a wry, impish smile that let us know that he knew that we knew that he didn't mean us.

Maurice refers to himself as a "*paysan*" and, in doing so, invokes a French stereotype close to an American "hick" or "bumpkin," someone ass-backwards in urban ways. Don't believe him. He also helped lead a ten-year battle to get Morbier, one of the cheeses he makes along with Comté, a protective AOC status from the French government. An AOC status, short for "*Appellation d'origine controlée*," means Morbier can be made only in the region and only under conditions that assure its quality. That means industry and a demand for export by ghouls like Chuck and me can't ruin his cheese. A David against the Goliaths of industry and bureaucracy, Maurice helped save Morbier.

We tasted it. Tangy, with a smack of bitter and soothe of cream, it gummed in the mouth as though it had half melted and, as we chewed, belted a hearth song of nut and hay. Maurice's Morbier is the best we've ever had.

*   *   *

"Glory be to God for dappled things," begins a poem by Gerard Manley Hopkins, and in his list of things—"skies of couple-colour," "finches' wings," "landscape plotted and pieced"—he includes "a brinded cow." I doubt Hopkins ever saw a Mont-béliarde, but that's the kind of cow he would have meant.

You don't expect them to be beautiful, especially when Maurice opens the small wooden door to the barn where his herd has been wintering for months, and you're hit with a blast of animal and shit. Your eyes feel coated. Your throat, too. You consider bolting from the cows you'd been so curious to see. And then you see them: at the trough, their huge heads placidly dipping into the dry, winter-green feed, their jaws working in a slow, steady rhythm. The grass and stems crunch as their large, pink-rimmed eyes look, maybe at you, maybe at nothing, and you look at them, at their bulk, their tagged ears that extend from their heads like scallops and twitch like insects, and at their color: mottled ginger, splotched with cream, beautiful, brinded, dappled things.

For a moment, you forget the shit. Until you hear what sounds close to a waterfall and you deduce the source. Yikes.

That splatter made Chuck, preened in her fur-collared vintage coat, reluctant to enter the pen, but when Maurice pulled back a dirt-smeared (was it dirt?) tarp, Chuck resolved to risk touching it and, in an act of sacrificial courage, entered.

The cows noticed. A few heads swung, a few lowered. Maybe the fur made her look or smell like some sort of predator. One cow took an interest. As it approached us, cautiously, stepping forward, then back, then forward, its delicacy surprised me. At 1,400 pounds, it placed its hooves carefully, as though it were stepping in large inkwells or practicing for a tap recital. The dancing cows in children's books now made sense. This Montbéliarde might just have jigged or hey-diddle-diddled except for the fact that the dead animal around Chuck's neck was freaking it out.

"The cows take on the character of their master," Maurice explained. A mean, aggressive master creates mean, aggressive beasts. A gentle master, gentle beasts.

Maurice never said he raises gentle beasts (though he did mention he has a few wily ones), but it's clear he does, from the shuffling cow in front of us, to the story he told us about how his cows trail him when he tries to leave them in the pastures, to the answer he gave us when Chuck asked him what he likes most about his work.

Maurice was showing us his two newest calves, who at a few days old were waist-high with the same brinded coats, though their fur was tufted and went in every direction, as if they'd been badly blow-dried or sculpted at a hip salon.

"*La chose vivante*," he finally said, after thinking about it for some time. The living thing. "I raised his mother and grandmother." He looked at one of the calves as though he could see the past in its skittish, unsteady movements. "Four generations. I take great pleasure in the living things."

Does *terroir* taste different when you're in that *terroir*?

The question that had taken us to the Jura recurred to me just before we left Maurice, when we were standing on his front steps. Chuck asked if we could see his pastures, and with a blackened nail he swept his hand across the woodsy hillsides that rose around Mesnay. They looked close, walkable, and if thirty-five heifers could hoof it up there, why couldn't Chuck and I? That was where the cheese began, in the dirt, and I wanted to see it, stand on it, X the spot in the map of my mind.

X turned out to be covered with muddy snow and rotten leaves.

A few hours later, Chuck and I found ourselves in a dark wood, halfway up a hill on which we'd seen, from the road below us, a church spire. That caught Chuck's attention, and since Maurice's sweep had taken in the horizon, we figured why not this hill? As soon as we started up, however, we lost sight of the cross and now we were ducking under branches and stepping through lichen-stippled pines that blocked our view and threw shadows on the path ahead. I couldn't imagine a cow managing the climb, not even a dancing one, but then cows don't wear their good leather shoes or go up in winter. My socks were squishy. When would the woods break into open, bonnie pastures?

I stopped to scrape the accumulated gook from my feet when Chuck's sniffer went off. She hooked the air in front of her with her nose, scrunched and unscrunched her nostrils.

"Smell it?" she said, in that way that usually means I won't. "It's the Morbier."

I craned my nose to a receptive angle and sniffed. I got pine, but pines were everywhere. I got old snow. I tried, but I didn't get Morbier.

"The rot," Chuck specified, bending to a clump of leaves

apparently left there for demonstration. She drew in a dragon's breath, held it, and smiled. "It's the same."

I stooped over the leaves. Sniffed. Sniffed again. Pictured the Morbier and stuck my nose on the muck. And I got it.

The muck still had hints of green hidden in it, and, as with the flavors of Morbier, I could sense a range of smells once I got past the hefty odor of decay, from seeded grass to wild marjoram. It seemed like I was tasting the ground.

And I was.

When you're in the *terroir*, you taste the *terroir*. Literally. That sounds odd, but it makes more sense after you take a fuller look at what it means to taste.

Imagine you're a Morbier.

You've been made and aged and cut and you're about to be eaten, but before that, while you're still a morsel not yet in a mouth, you're already releasing molecules that waft into the nose of whoever is about to eat you and that dissolve in their mucus.

Yuck, you might think, but you're Morbier and you don't think. Besides, these molecules you've released—minute airborne chemicals that scientists call "odors"—have reached the odor receptors in your eater's nose. Each odor that you give off has a particular shape, and that shape matches a particular odor receptor in the nose, the way a key matches a lock. Now, when your odor "key" hits a nose receptor's "lock," it triggers a neuron to send a signal from the nose to the brain. Once this signal reaches the brain, it combines with other signals "unlocked" by other odors, and the brain uses them to create the experience we know as "taste."

You've probably heard that taste is mostly smell, and that's true. Eighty to ninety percent of tasting happens through our sense of smell, but the odors that you taste don't all have to come from the food you're tasting. They can come from freshly cut grass (think of the smell a lawn mower unleashes) or wildflowers (think of a lavender bush) or a bunch of rotting, moldy leaves (think of a muddy hillside in Mesnay). Tasting means tasting more than what's in your mouth. Tasting involves every odor that enters your nostrils, and if those odors come from the same place in which your Morbier was made, then you're not only tasting the *terroir* in the cheese, but also the *terroir* that surrounds you, in the air, on the ground, up the nose. You taste the place in which you taste.

That tasting doesn't stop after you've taken a bite. As you chew, you release more molecules that float up the back of your throat, where they hit your odor receptors and trigger your neurons to signal your brain. Your nose never stops. It's what lets you experience thousands of different tastes.

Your mouth gives you just five. That doesn't mean you don't need it. It releases more flavor-creating molecules for you to smell. It also helps you taste salty, sweet, sour, bitter, and savory.

Let's say you're a Morbier again and now you're being mashed up inside a mouth. Teeth are breaking you down, saliva is breaking you down, a tongue is mushing you around, and you're releasing molecules. Not all of them are floating up the nose of whoever is eating you. They're also hitting little raised bumps called "papillae" on the top of this person's tongue, soft palate, and throat. Many of them look like weird mushrooms or strange sea anemones with outstretched tentacles. Some house taste buds, small bundles of cells that work similarly to the odor receptors in the nose: They detect chemical molecules or "tastants" from the cheese and, when they do, trigger a neuron to send a signal to the brain. The brain receives these signals and figures out whether you taste salty, sweet, sour, bitter, or savory, and the person who's eating you either spits you out or takes another bite.

So, if you were a Morbier, you'd begin as cheese, but soon you'd become molecules that combined with other molecules in the air and you'd start triggering reactions in sense receptors that cause neurons to fire along the cranial nerves until, as clusters of signals, you finally reached the most miraculous thing that has ever existed, the human brain, which would receive you, decode you, and turn you and the *terroir* around you into a taste.

The human brain also hatches fantasies, and a few days after tasting that Mesnay hillside, Chuck and I cracked a favorite: Marcel Petite's Comté from the Fort Saint-Antoine.

To start, I should say that Comté has our vote for world's most versatile cheese. Stilton's veined blues hit creamier heights, old wheels of Parmigiano-Reggiano hold more *gravitas*, and Vacherin, with its cloud-rippled rind, has more of heaven in it, but none of these are cheeses you can eat every day. They're more like arias or Botticellis, shaking your palate into awe with their beauty. They transport you, engulf you, but they also leave you agasp and spent. You need to recover. You couldn't snack on a Stilton throughout the afternoon or stash some Parm or Vacherin in your handbag to nibble on during an endless commute. These cheeses enrapture you the way a diva does.

Not so with Comté. A little black dress of a cheese, Comté flatters almost any moment, any mood. Want a breakfast that makes the flavors sing in plain black coffee? Comté. Want a dessert to follow the cherry-drizzled lamb and rosemary-spiked potatoes you're serving to your judgmental mother-in-law? Comté. Want to turn a cigarette break into a gourmet escape? Comté.

Comté is the world's most versatile cheese because it has more than a hundred possible flavors, from leather, apricot, pepper, mushroom, soil, tobacco, leek, and almond, to choco-late, whey, fried onion, honeydew, cauliflower, and cave, to plum, vanilla, beef broth, endive, brioche, wildflower, horse, and fudge. You could eat it, as Maurice has, every day of your life and every day you'd eat well. Of the world's best cheeses, Comté pleases most.

And Marcel Petite's Comté from the Fort Saint-Antoine is the most pleasing Comté that Chuck and I have ever tasted. We had it first in Cambridge, where it has pride of place at Formaggio, and it went off in our mouths like a sparkler or a sudden rush of joy. Chuck's smile linked her earlobes, and I had the simultaneous urge to keep it on my tongue forever, so I could savor every slowly emerging taste, and to devour the entire eighty-pound wheel. That, to me, defines it. Comté yields the rare complexity and delicacy of flavors you find in the most superior cheeses, but it also sates that desire for gut-sticking food, the sort you want after shoveling snow or crying or visiting vegans. It won both my inner cheese snob and child at once. How?

I asked our monger, and that's when Chuck and I learned of "Le Fort," the stuff of cheese fantasy.

"Are those stalactites?" Chuck asked, gawking at the ceiling high above us.

We had just entered the Fort, and the daggers that hovered above us in a perpetual drip signaled that, despite the Fort's modest exterior, we weren't in any ordinary cheese cave.

Outside, the Fort merges with the forest around it. The gray, rust-speckled stones that form its front wall seem more natural than manmade, and the heavy snow that tops it runs smoothly into the nearby thickets of pine and spruce. To reach its huge doors, you cross a footbridge that evokes moats and castles, a princess trapped in a high tower.

Yet, the size of what you see isn't that impressive and certainly isn't high. Above ground, the Fort looks as though it would make for a glorious stable or root cellar, but a fort? It has a squat, unimposing shape, like a utility building at an old prison or defunct quarry. If you imagined a nineteenth-century Prussian army marching upon it, you'd hear their snickers. ("Fort, vhat fort?") Luckily for the Jurassians, this possibility, for which Général Séré de Rivières and a fleet of masons, soldiers, and stonecutters built the fort in 1879, never happened. Instead, new advances in artillery quickly made the fort obsolete—its stones would crumble against the shell blasts that riddled the Great War—and it fell into disuse.

It took a genius to see in this useless relic the future of Comté, and, in 1966, Marcel Petite convinced the French government to let him turn the Fort into a cheese cave. Petite built a roof over the Fort's courtyard, heaped twenty-six feet of earth on top of the roof, and filled the Fort with three hundred wheels of Comté. Now, forty-plus years later, it houses 65,000. And the fact that they're underground means that what you see when you approach it gives you the wrong impression of what you'll see once you're inside it.

The stalactites that Chuck spotted gave us our first glimpse into the real nature of this subterranean cheesescape.

"Oui," nodded Laetitia, smiling.

Our guide, Laetitia, struck us as extremely cool. She had blonde hair that spiked out stylishly, if unstyled, and framed her grinning eyes and designer glasses. She also had less body fat than celery.

Chuck found this lankiness a bit off-putting. Not because she hasn't made peace with a certain amount of softness, but because of the cheese clothes that Laetitia made us wear. Gauzy thin and lab white, the coats are meant to keep the aging cave clean. When Chuck got hers, she went to take off her fox fur coat.

"Oh, no," insisted Laetitia. "You'll be much too cold."

Chuck sized up the cheese coat. With a second coat inside it, the fit wasn't going to be flattering. She gave me a glance, and I shrugged. We were visitors, compelled by decorum. Chuck pressed her lips together and, a squirrel wriggling into a tube sock, forced herself into the cheese coat. It wasn't unflattering. It was worse. Her huge fox-fur cuffs and huger fox-fur collar stretched the coat to a monstrous size. She looked like an Oompa-Loompa, a red-headed Humpty. In France. In front of a Frenchwoman.

"Here's your hat," said Laetitia, her own cheese coat fitting trimly over her svelte down vest.

Thrust into the ugly pit, Chuck stuffed her hair into the white cap, which lumped in more odd directions, and the two of us, transformed into hygienically clad ogres, followed Laetitia into the stony guts of the Fort.

The sun is gone.

You see, dimly, by the sepulchral light that coats the walls and arches, as the endless rows of cheese stretch, wheel after wheel, into shadow. The scale isn't human. The distances are too vast, the shelves of Comté too high.

Craning your head straight up, you wonder who looks after the highest wheels, and soon you see your answer, in the Comté robot working its way down another aisle. It looks boxy and dronish, no Wall-E or R2-D2 whisking around with cheery clicks and anthropomorphizing whistles. It prongs up a wheel, pulls it into its center, squirts it with a salt-water wash, scrubs it with a thickly bristled brush, flips it, squirts and scrubs it again, then slides it back, before moving to the next cheese, and the next, forever. It looks plucked from the future, as do the uniformed workers who hover on carts across the wet floor.

And yet the original Fort, the rock all around you that looks more slapped together than finely hewn, makes you

expect Général Séré de Rivière will swagger out of a Dumas novel and around the next corner. You can picture his impressive hat and tasseled shoulders.

Then again, as you toe down the shallow, unlit stairs, with the huff of ammonia in your nose, you might also bump into a hooded monk or toothless guildsman, since the collective making of Comté goes back centuries, and the wheels themselves, with their rough hides and milk, rose, and rust colors, resemble the wheels on a donkey cart. When they reach their moldiest, they have a whitish coat of mold and break out in small bulbous protrusions. They look plague struck.

So, the medieval past and the techno future merge in a commercial present, where the working model comes from Ford's assembly line, and you ask how this place, where time twists back on itself and space unravels, can make such amazing Comté?

The prospect seems more improbable since the Fort feels desolate. A few workers pass you with a "Bonjour," not that you'd know whether it was *jour* or *soir*. It could be three in the morning. And the robot does have a presence, not that you'd consider it companionable. On the whole, though, entire sections of the Fort, old armories and wide balconies, are empty except for the cheese. In the room where the Comté wheels arrive, a blowtorch used to brand the wheels burns unattended, its blue flame hissing into the emptiness.

After an hour in the Fort, winding through its high stacks and hearing your steps echo off the damp stones, you feel like the last patron in a great abandoned library or a servant buried in the tomb of an Egyptian pharaoh, charged to watch over his earthly riches as he journeys into the next world.

*   *   *

With the hundred mix-and-match flavors in Comté to choose from, meeting the impassive stare of a professional Comté taster who has just plugged a wheel and handed you a sample can be daunting. And if that taster is Sylvan, whose name and character harkens back to Silvanus, a god of the forest, then watching as he tastes the cheese before you, registers but doesn't say the right answer, then looks at you with expectant eyes—a slightly cruel twinkle in them—can be plain scary. In myth, mortals who square off against gods never fare well.

Sometimes, I thought to myself, it's nice not to have French.

Chuck has French. And as we chewed, she looked to Laetitia for support. Maybe she'd toss out an adjectival lifeline. But Laetitia's face was as blank as Sylvan's. Later, when Sylvan had warmed to Chuck, he would explain that they preferred to hear our "brute perspective." It interested them to see what our rough palates took from their exquisite cheese.

Warmth, however, wasn't what Chuck was feeling at this moment. Scrutiny, perhaps. Inadequacy, for sure.

"Milk," she finally said, which is a braver choice than it might seem, since all cheese is made of milk. In hazarding this flavor, Chuck risked a dismissive "*Bien sûr*." How obvious.

"*Oui!*" boomed Sylvan, his chiseled features leaping into delight and his arms snapping out in crisp, affirmative bursts. He then unloosened his unbrute perspective in French I couldn't follow. Nonetheless, as I listened to him, Chuck, and Laetitia talk through the Comté's milky flavor, I did understand what had happened: Chuck had pleased the god.

From that "oui," tasting became easier each time Sylvan took us through the ritual. It began with Sylvan jerking out a wheel and whacking it systematically with a small mallet so he could listen—*listen*—for cracks and fissures inside the cheese. As he hammered, he looked as though he desperately wanted to provoke a reflexive kick from a giant's kneecap. Then he'd flip the mallet, which has a hollow handle, and twist it into the wheel. When he pulled it back out, it would hold a "plug" of Comté, from which he'd break off a piece, squish it between his fingers, sniff it, and pop it in his mouth. Bang. In an instant, he'd have the flavor profile. Then, without a word, he'd offer some of the plug to us, and we'd follow his lead: break, squish, sniff, and pop. It always ended the same way, with Chuck guessing into the Comté void.

She was right about half the time, and once was quickly informed that a cheese she praised for its rarefied depth was, in fact, "*sauvage*." Still, fifty-fifty isn't so bad for a brute battling a god.

The question haunted me: How can making 65,000 of anything result in anything good?

As I marveled at the shelves of Comté towering around me, I couldn't see how so much product didn't lead to a mass-produced blandness, especially when the Fort ran on such a skeletal crew. For me, this Comté was art, but how do you make art on such a scale?

Chuck put this question to Laetitia and Sylvan early on, and gradually we pieced together the answer.

It starts in the villages, where farmers like Maurice gather the milk for Comté. Farmers do milk and only milk. Once they've got it, they pool it with other farmers from the same village whose cows have grazed in the same pastures and send it to a "*fruitier*," where it gets made into Comté.

The term "*fruitier*" goes back to 1272 and refers to the "common fruit" of Jurassic farmers who combine their milk to make big cheeses. *Fruitiers* do cheesemaking and only cheesemaking. They take the farmers' milk and turn it, 118 gallons at a time, into wheels of Comté. The *fruitiers* know every detail of the milk—the time of milking, the state of the cows, the nature of the feed—and use this knowledge to coax out the milk's flavors. The *fruitiers* and farmers stay in daily contact, which results in wheels of Comté as bound to the *terroir* as the cows grazing in the nearby pastures.

Once the *fruitiers* make the wheels, they care for them over the next few weeks, salting and turning them while the cheese is still "green" ("green cheese" means "fresh or new cheese," and it's very white), but the main work of aging happens after the *fruitier* sends the cheese to a cave, where *affineurs* like Sylvan attend to it for eight to thirty-six months. *Affineurs* do aging and only aging. They know the *fruitiers*, as well as the conditions their wheels need to develop, and through salting, turning, moving, monitoring, and constantly "plugging" the cheese, *affineurs* bring each wheel to its peak. Only then do they send it to the mongers who sell it to us.

Sixty-five thousand wheels of Comté can taste so good because making Comté is really three kinds of making— milk-making, cheesemaking, and cheese aging—and that division leaves each maker free to perfect his part. And to

do more of it. Comté makers join together to do what they couldn't do alone.

That's how Chuck and I planned to tackle Mont d'Or, as a team, as attuned to each other as a farmer, *fruitier*, and *affineur*.

We were dead set on making the summit and, to get there, to scale its terrible height, we were prepared to ride the ski lift as far as it would hoist us, and if the lift didn't hoist us to the top, why then, by God, we'd walk. We had boots. We had baggies of gorp that Chuck had assembled in Cambridge and stuffed with semisweet chocolate. We had long underwear that bunched up like baby diapers.

First, however, we had to have lunch. We couldn't ascend Mont d'Or before we'd eaten a Vacherin Mont d'Or. So, with the sun sharp in the afternoon sky and the Mont awaiting us, we ducked into a sleepy restaurant in the skiing village of Métabief and perused the menu.

"*Bôite chaude!*" Chuck shrieked, much as Archimedes must have when he watched the water rise in his bath and cried "Eureka!"

Chuck had found it: the "hot box" over which we'd salivated since we'd read about it months earlier, online and unattainable. A *bôite chaude* begins with a gooey, ooey, absolutely lovely Vacherin still tucked in its small spruce box. You open its center, pour in a little Jurassic white wine, and add a scatter of garlic that's gnarly and growling from the long winter. Then you put the top back on the box, wrap the whole thing in foil, and slide it into a fiery oven until the garlic and wine saturate the whole cheese, and the Vacherin devolves into a runny, slightly browned mess. To serve it, you slather it on heaps of steamed potatoes that you split open seconds before you eat them so that curls of steam dance from them like tipsy spirits. Chuck is Irish. Potatoes trigger a genetic need in her. Potatoes drowned in winey, garlicky Vacherin might very well collapse her double helixes.

We ordered two.

Our waiter, a busty mountain woman with the girth of a Hummer and, in her tangerine blouse, the chic of a supermodel, said one was enough for two. We double-checked. She assured us. We consented and watched the pendulum-hinged door to the kitchen swing back and forth, back and forth, for a breathless half hour.

The hot box finally arrived, perched atop a wooden hutch with a tiny door that housed a dozen potatoes. We ate it, and them, and the sheets of *jambon de pays* that came with them, and the Morteau sausages, and the leathery *jambon cru*, and the sweet cornichons that perk up the palate and unlock the second stomach, and the one, then two thick carafes of Jurassic savagnin. We scraped the last of the *bôite chaude* out of the box with our fingertips.

We had a mountain to climb.

The reality of the *bôite chaude* surpassed our fantasy. Our climb did not.

In fact, from the moment we bloated out of the restaurant to the moment we stood on the summit of Mont d'Or, sweaty and crampy and with melted snow in our boots, reality didn't much figure into our trek.

The fantasy I'll call Chuck and I Perish on the Mountain of Gold and Aren't Found, If Ever, Until the Spring Thaw and It's Your Fault, Why Didn't You Listen to Me, You Madman began when we saw the sun had moved considerably since we'd left it for lunch. The light had that late-afternoon intensity that sears and mutes what it hits.

Chuck's torso tilted skyward. "Do you think we have time?" she asked, more of the sky than me.

My gut jagged, and not from the sausage. Chuck's voice had a note of foreboding I'd heard before, when she spots a wormhole in her apple or when she isn't sure she's heard the supposedly vacuum-sealed lid on the salsa jar pop. Here, however, we had traveled 3,661 miles on money we didn't have over a few days we'd ripped from our calendars, all so we could climb a fantasy we'd found inside a cheese. I thought we should soldier on.

"We can make it," I said, preemptively hooking Chuck's elbow and aiming us at the ski lift.

"What time is it?"

I could hear the worry swelling as I dragged Chuck after me. My haste didn't matter. The fantasy of Chuck and me perishing grew in Chuck's mind with every encounter: The snarly ski bunny who sold us our lift tickets told her it would take two hours for us to reach Mont d'Or after we rode up. Apparently it sat on the far side of Mont Morond, the mountain that had the lift. She also said the lift would stop in two hours and, *absolument*, no walking down. We weren't allowed up, no she wouldn't even sell us the tickets, unless we had good boots.

In a blink, Chuck saw us stranded on the mountainside, in the dark, dying, in our good boots.

"We can at least go up for a look," I bargained after Chuck had translated the snarly bunny's admonishments. If I could get her up there, maybe we'd find the situation wasn't so bad. "We can at least see it."

"Okay," said soldier Chuck, not sounding okay, "I guess we can *see* it."

"You can't see it from here."

The ski instructor wasn't as snarly as the snarly ski bunny, but he wasn't helpful, either.

We'd made it to the top of Mont Morond, swept up its piney slopes by the lift as our boots dangled above skiers who shot down the trails below us like neon comets. More skiers littered the peak. They wove around us as we clambered out of the thoroughfare and made our way to the wooden shack that looked vaguely official. That's where we found the ski instructor. He let us know, with a chin nod, that Mont d'Or was thataway, toward a hump of rocks in the middle distance and that it took two, maybe three hours to walk it.

Chuck gave me the news with a sigh of relief: We had no hope of making it, so we had no need to try. The facts had spared her. She almost smiled.

"Ask him if we can see it from the hump," I asked her.

Chuck's almost-smile receded, and her tight-lipped purse

returned. She asked, against her will, and learned that we could see Mont d'Or from the hump.

"Ask him how we get there," I pressed, pretending I didn't see the plead in Chuck's eyes.

She swallowed and turned back to the ski instructor. "What path do we take to get there?"

"There's no path," he informed her. "Go toward those trees and keep going."

The blood in Chuck's lips disappeared. No path. No path and no time and no way back down if we didn't find our way back along the no-path in no-time. Chuck had fought valiantly, but at last her dark fantasy enveloped her. The sun might have been shining, the mountainside might have been full of skiers, the gravest danger we might have faced might have been walking a few miles down a ski trail to our parked Prius, but none of this reality registered for Chuck. She saw death on those far rocks. Fantasy infused her sight.

In this, Chuck is like us all. We tend to think that reality exists apart from what we imagine about it, that the raw world lies separate from our cooked views of it. That's why we love blind tastings, in which a Burgundian *grand cru* goes up against a Jersey swill, and four out of five tasters prefer the swill. We believe that the truth about the wine has emerged. We might have been snookered by the fantasies that those labels foisted on us, but through the blind tasting, reality has been revealed. We now taste the wine in the raw.

Yet, when neuroscientists put us in an MRI and watch what happens to our brains as we taste, this take on reality and fantasy doesn't hold up. What we imagine about what we taste changes our neural response to it. If we know that we're tasting a *grand cru*, our brain lights up differently—the reality of our experience is different—than if we taste exactly the same *grand cru* without knowing it's a *grand cru*. There aren't any raw or real tastes, any things in themselves, free from our cooked views of them. Our thoughts, expectations, and imaginings don't obscure the reality of what we're tasting; they shape it.

So, however odd or oddly formed, those fantasies we have about delectating Vacherin Mont d'Or at the foot of Mont d'Or or risking death to reach its peak, those fantasies infuse our experience of the cheese, of the Mont, really.

The largest rock in the hump of rocks turned out to be Mont d'Or.

A steel plaque informed us of this fact not far from what we now knew was the summit, and we looked on it with new eyes. Its stony bulk jutted into the sky like the flat fist of a giant, and the wind that struck it leapt from it, as though it were too hostile a place to rest. Eddies of snow spun into the air. Behind it, sunlit and vast, the Alps rose as a jagged spine, and below it, we could see stenciled villages and forests that spread thickly from the white fields in all directions.

Having given up hope of it before we started, we were, we realized, going to reach the top of Mont d'Or. For a moment, Chuck stopped worrying, and we stood there together.

Then we walked up.

On the Mountain of Gold, you stand above the pines that grow straight at you from the cliffs below and punctu-

ate the rock. On the Mountain of Gold, you step carefully, though you're not sure why, and you see more mountains that you know you'll never climb along horizons you know you'll never cross. On the Mountain of Gold, you hang over the snowy lip of the world and you wonder how a cheese could have led you so far, so high—because that's how you got here, isn't it?—and you feel lucky to be alive.

Chuck's Picks

———

The title of this appendix might seem antithetical, for our author would have you believe that I, Chuck, cannot manage to pick at all. You may remember him recounting me, frozen with choice, before the great cheese wall at Formaggio Kitchen. For Chuck, he tells you, choice is "a torment."

To a certain extent, he's right. Oh, he certainly likes to torment me with the memory of a frigid February day in Paris, when we wandered across four arrondissements looking for the perfect Napoleon (which the French, who first made it, call "*mille-feuilles*"). I remember his encouraging words, in front of every window, "Isn't this one good enough?" because it was very cold, and we were in Paris, and what did a pastry matter anyway?

But *mille-feuilles* is a precarious pastry, requiring a precise balance of sweet to crisp to crème. One does not get many chances to enjoy one's favorite pastry in the world's most romantic city with one's beloved. An inferior *mille-feuilles* would have squandered the chance. So, we wandered for hours, getting colder and increasingly more jaw-clenched, only to end up back at one of the very first pâtisseries we'd passed, purchasing a *mille-feuilles* I'd initially rejected for some unremembered flaw and yet which turned out to be perfectly delicious.

Eric often recalls this experience as a cautionary tale. Today, when my eyes look away from the cheese at hand, wondering if a better cheese waits around the bend, he speaks the word "Napoleon," recalling that cold day and calling me to settle for "good enough."

However, he's missed the *real* moral of the story. The moral of the *mille-feuilles* is that I, Chuck, can enjoy the Napoleon at hand only when we've exhausted all the other options. If we'd bought that exact same pastry on the first pass, the shadow Napoleons waiting in better pâtisseries on roads not taken would have haunted every bite. In truth, it would not have been the same Napoleon at all. The one that was merely "good enough" three hours earlier could delight us only when we knew that it was the best of all the *mille-feuilles* Paris had to offer. The moral of the *mille-feuilles* is that "good enough" is never good enough, until it's the best you can find.

So while Eric is right to say that choice is something of a torment for me, I have to clarify that it's nothing to the torment of settling for "good enough." So I weigh and walk and debate and double-back and agonize and overanalyze, but then I finally—despite what Eric might lead you to believe— choose. And when I choose, I know, à la Candide, that this choice is the best of all possible choices.

In the pages that follow, I've aimed to endure the tor- ment of choice for you. How many chances do you get to put together a top-notch cheese plate? To indulge in luxurious Jamón Ibérico? To buy a wine beyond the everyday budget?

These moments can't be wasted. They matter too much, as a Napoleon in Paris matters too much. So, I've done my best to brave the agonies of choice, of weeding good enough from best there is, in the hopes of sparing you the torment. I've also suggested, along the way, some principles I've found helpful in creating pairings, in case they'll assist you in making your own choices.

This appendix might be more aptly named "Chuck's Agonizingly Debated Selections of the Most Delicious Treats You Can Eat and Drink with the Cheeses that, Out of All the Cheeses You Might Choose, You Should Choose, If You Only Got One Chance to Choose." Eric encouraged me to call it "Chuck's Picks." It's less telling as a title, but I suppose it's good enough.

BEER

I fear that I am not awesome enough to drink beer.

I used to believe that beer was the drink of the many, myself included. This belief stemmed in part from beer's presence at ballparks, stadiums, concert halls, racetracks, corner bars, and other places where we, the many, gather. Mostly this belief stemmed from an odder source, my reading of nineteenth-century novels. Thomas Hardy, George Eliot, throughout their novels' pages, mowers take a break from their mowing, growers from their growing, to gather in the shade of a fine tree at the edge of fragrant fields, where they break out homely bread and hunks of cheese and refresh themselves with beer. Seeking that pastoral refreshment, I visited several pubs featuring a ploughman's lunch, yet the Newcastle or Smithwicks I ordered alongside it never tasted so idyllically nourishing as the brews I'd imagined in those fields. Still, my belief remained that beer was about shade trees and sweaty brows, noble labor, neighborly affection, and every other splendid cliché robed in sentimentality that make me love nineteenth-century novels. (I later learned that those workers drank beer because it was more hygienic and safe than the water they had access to, yet that reality was so unsentimental that it simply could not overturn my long-held *Adam Bede* beer fantasy.) Beer was honest, hardworking, and friendly.

But beer, since George Eliot first whetted my taste for it, has become cool.

Yes, George Eliot's serge-wearing yeomen gave way in my mind, about a year ago, to Dan Thompkins. Dan is the beer guy for the Bueno Queso Social Club, the monthly foodie gathering Eric and I attend. Don't let his workaday name fool you, Dan is about as rocking as they come: facial piercings, ear plugs, tattoos, shaved head, centaur-styled goatee. He's got a lot of metal, on garments and limbs. Whether he actually has the words "love" and "hate" tattooed on his knuckles or merely might, I can't say. The point is that if you are anything like me, you would expect to be mocked, not offered tasting advice, from this extremely hip and slightly threatening-looking guy.

Because of and beyond the metal, Dan has completely transformed my sense of beer. He's no Adam Bede, that's clear. Moreover, month after month, Dan has picked beers so interesting, so complex, so delicious that they've consistently outperformed the wines another of the hosts chose to pair with that day's cheeses.

Dan will whip out a Saint Boltoph's Town Rustic Dark Ale from Pretty Things Beer and wax about malts roasted in coal-fired drums, or he'll crack the Pozharnik Espresso Russian Imperial Stout, from Pennichuck Brewing, and tell how it's brewed with coffee and vanilla beans and aged in whiskey barrels. Both beers taste as astonishing as they sound. Through their flavors, I've come to understand that beer can be a lot more like Dan than like the straightforward laborers who populate Eliot's stories: In other words, beer can be surprising, engaging, and more than a little bit strange.

Take Innis & Gunn Oak Aged Beer. It tastes of whisky, yet has the bubble of beer, yet imparts the fragrance of wine.

At once thick and crisp, the beer might cloy your tongue from its oakiness, if not for the bubbles; it might overwhelm you with malt, if not for the fruit. This beer is a conundrum. And it becomes more puzzling still when you add cheese, for then it pulls deep nuances out of the cheese, nuances of wheat and hearth, even as the cheese simultaneously mellows the beer. Pairing cheese with this beer makes it at once more and less complex. And, while it's amazing that you can pair so complex a beer with anything, yet it seems to go with everything. A conundrum indeed.

Another genre-bending beer is the Flemish-style red called Duchesse de Bourgogne from Brouwerij Verhaeghe. The woman on the label (medieval or Vermeeresque, I'm not sure) looks smug, as if she's smirking in advance at the surprise you're about to have. She's right. In a blind tasting, I probably couldn't even identify what it is. Wine? Sangria? Sherry? Beer would be low on the guess list. It's sour, but in a pleasing sort of way, especially once you add a cheese. Pairing this beer with young goat cheeses is fascinating, for the two sournesses start to gang up together, threatening to topple the beer into gross, but then the cream in the cheese and the fruit in the beer, like calming parental influences, merge it into a pleasurable whole.

Evidently, Dan chases interesting beers. He was recently on the hunt for a fermented brew reconstructed from a residue in an excavated Egyptian tomb.

Now, the hard truth is that I am simply not radical enough to enjoy some of the more esoteric selections that Dan and other beer professionals find worthwhile. A lambic like Girardin Gueuze 1882 from Belgium gives me the shivers. But while some of his selections have been beyond me, Dan has shown me how flexible and friendly beers can be with cheese.

A beer like Cisco Brewers' Whale's Tale Pale Ale from Nantucket—while perhaps more everyday than Dan's adventurous choices—highlights the primary gift that beers bring to cheese. This beer is clean, flavorful, and has bubbles. I don't add this final attribute lightly: Bubbles are key. Through carbonation, beer zips into the fat on your tongue much the way champagne does, cleansing and clearing it away, to let you return fresh to the cheese. Bewitched by beer's bubbles, I have, on many occasions, eaten more cheese than was good for me. The Whale's Tale Pale Ale is infinitely refreshing, it's a breeze, and so you return, infinitely refreshed, to the cheese.

A hoppier beer like Duchy Originals Organic English Ale refreshes less, but plays more with whatever cheese you throw at it. The hops in the beer cling to whatever is in your mouth, pouncing on the cheese and pulling at it with their sticky, bitter grip. If you give this beer a sturdy enough cheese to romp with, the interplay will be quite volatile. Perhaps its strength of character comes from its royal lineage: This ale is made for HRH the Prince of Wales himself and includes hops taken from the Home Farm at Highgrove.

The English Ale suggests, in its origin, one obvious pairing for beers of all origins: English cheeses. Since England has no wine-producing region, English cheeses (unlike most European cheeses) were never intended to be paired with wine. Cheddar and wine just seems weird. From a grows together goes together standpoint, **Cheddar, Kirkham's Lancashire,**

Lincolnshire Poacher, Red Leicester, Double Gloucester, Stilton, and all the other Jane Austen cheeses will shine with beer.

Thus it happened that, with a grassy hunk of **Mrs. Appleby's Cheshire** on my plate and a saison farmhouse ale warming in my glass, I met the flavors of those long-dreamt-of luncheons from the fields of a nineteenth-century shire. And though I sat on a Sunday afternoon in a nightclub on Mass Ave, where the buses' air brakes screeched through the window, and though my glass held ales from Belgium and Colorado, and though Dan was not an honest yeoman with a care-worn face and a sturdy trust in providence, nevertheless, the grass in the cheese mingled with the malted barley in the glass, and there was a lilt of freshly cut grass in the wind or my imagination. And I thought: Beer and cheese are awesome.

Cheeses to Have with Beer

My favorite beer-pairing cheeses tend to fall into the grass-butter-nut-caramel flavor family. The more citric, yogurt-flavored cheeses don't meet beer as merrily as those with nutty, warm tones. Happily, that winning flavor range leaves open cheese's whole array of formats and styles.

The style I'd most immediately pair with beer is cooked, pressed cheeses. The majority of the famous English cheeses fall into this camp and so they suggest other successful choices. **Wilde Weide,** a Gouda-style cow's milk cheese from Holland, is fantastic with a crisp amber ale. The cheese tastes like a collision of trees and salted caramels. With beer, it's intoxicating.

Washed rind cheeses can also flourish alongside beer. This too makes sense, since many a washed rind cheese is actually washed *with* beer. **Timberdoodle,** from Vermont, has just the right kind of stink to mix with beer's inherent bitterness. This cheese never swerves toward rot or rank, but sits pleasantly at salty and suggestive. With a hoppier beer, like the Duchy Originals Organic English Ale, Timberdoodle's slight stink becomes enjoyable, and you'll wonder why you don't eat more washed rind cheeses. So too, the French mixed-milk, washed rind **Trois Laits** harmonizes well with beer, especially wheat beer, since its yeasty tones are a natural match.

And finally, a surprising third family for pairing may well be the most enjoyable of them all: Semi-firm cow's milk cheese, like the Piedmontese **Nostrale di Elva** or the gnarlier **Tomme Crayeuse** from Savoie, offers a rich chance for beer to show just how far it can go in stepping up to cheese. The thick *pâte* in these cheeses is literally and figuratively so pliable it issues an open invitation to whatever accompanies it. Nostrale di Elva, in particular, has always reminded me of that shopworn, yet beloved character of many a novel: the good-natured tart. She's so joyous, bawdy, and high-spirited, she pleases uniformly. Paired with an Adam Bede of an ale, who knows what mischief or delight the two together will create?

CHOCOLATE

To pair cheese and chocolate might sound a bit like pairing wine and beer, coffee and tea. These pairs are more often treated as adversaries than chums. You're probably more likely to choose whether to enjoy coffee *or* tea with breakfast, wine *or* beer with dinner, than to deliberate which coffee best highlights the delicate characteristics of the white tea you'll be enjoying alongside it. Chocolate and cheese suffer the same alienation. Mostly they stare at each other from opposite sides of the meal experience: Cheese bookends the start as an hors d'œuvre, chocolate the end as dessert. On Euro-inspired menus, cheese can sometimes join chocolate as a dessert alternative, but this rapprochement brings the two no closer to companionship, since it only pits them against each other. Cheese plate *or* profiteroles, we debate, since we'd feel a glutton to choose the cheese plate *and* profiteroles.

Welcome to a world in which you can have cheese and chocolate together. The trick to pairing the two *sans* gluttony lies in choosing chocolate that tastes more of rain forests than of Hansel and Gretel's forest cottage. If you were to try waxy, highly sweetened name-brand chocolates with cheese, you'd get a combination that tasted something like cream cheese brownies and chocolate cheesecake—essentially a blend of savory fat and sweet fat. However, chocolate that tastes of place and plant can draw surprising flavors from cheeses made a hemisphere and a climate change away.

Chocolate, after all, starts in plants, in seed-bearing trees from rain forests around the equator. This organic origin makes chocolate as natural a playmate for cheese as those more familiar fruit-based companions: wine, dried fruit, olives, preserves. The elaborate process in which raw cacao is transformed into chocolate just obscures the leafy origin of the bar. In brief: Huge cacao pods (shaped like groovy over-sized mangos) are macheted from the trunk of the cacao tree and cracked to reveal forty or so seeds coated in a viscous, white, pulpy material called "baba." The seeds and baba are scooped out, carted away by donkeys, and fermented for a time in banana leaves. The fermented seeds, once dried, then head to the factory, where they are roasted and win-nowed to reveal the individual "nibs" that make up each bean. Finally, the nibs are ground into a cacao liquor, which can be manipulated with vanilla, sugar, milk, and other fla-vors, then powdered or molded into the concoction we eat as chocolate.

Pod to baba to bean to nib to liquor to bar, the whole process seems too complex and unlikely, I wonder how it came about. Pictures of the process only make it the more bizarre and oddly terrifying: Images of baba-ensconced beans vaguely recall a sci-fi film, in which clowns or aliens or alien clowns cocoon their victims in pods spun of a white baba-like substance, then eat, kill, or gestate them into killers of their kind. The recent proliferation of organic, high cacao content, and single-origin chocolate bars makes the plant beginnings of chocolate much easier to believe. Even better, these bars make that origin pos-sible to taste.

To taste the plant at the root of chocolate, you can go directly to the source: A Massachusetts chocolate company named Taza sells roasted, whole cacao nibs, which give a nearly unadulterated taste of the raw material that becomes the chocolate bar. A roasted nib looks a bit like a legless ant and feels dry and gritty, like crumbling a burnt peanut shell between your teeth. The taste too is acrid and slightly bitter, how the inside of a peach pit might taste. Yet, even as the sides of your throat pull together in revolt, your brain triggers with hints of chocolatey magic, a dust of earth, a lift of fragrance. You'd never pop a handful of these like M&M's, but you can see how M&M's came about.

Having indulged in precisely two ant-sized nibbles of nibs, I'd recommend the experience to anyone. I'd also recommend trying the nibs alongside one of Taza's Mexicano bars. The combination helps you pick the raw cacao flavor out of the more processed medley of the chocolate bar. Calling Taza's Mexicano bars "processed," however, feels like an overstatement, particularly in comparison to familiar name-brand chocolates. Those bars almost always involve a process called "conching," which smoothes out the chocolate mixture to give it a glossy, uniform texture. Taza's bars are unique in being stone-ground and unconched, which means that the cacao nibs, cane sugar, vanilla beans, cinnamon sticks, chilies, or almonds are simply tossed onto huge stone *molinos* ("mills") and ground together. The result is a chocolate that retains a granulated texture in which sugar sparkles like flecks of mica from the base of grainy cacao nibs. Made this way, the Mexicano bar is essentially a sweeter, more generous experience that still recalls the education of cracking cacao nibs between your teeth.

Now, for the real adventure: Add some cheese. The goat's milk **Pawlet,** made by Peter Dixon at Consider Bardwell Farm, will bring a creamy caramel warmth to the cacao's earthy dryness. For a dessert-inspired pairing, eat the Pawlet with Taza's cinnamon bar: Caramel, cinnamon, chocolate, and cream blend into a savory sundae on your tongue. Or you could taste the Pawlet with Taza's Guajillo Chili bar. The slow heat of the chilies spreading through the sweetness of cheese and cacao will hint not at dessert, but dinner, enchiladas with *mole*. Or, for a snack, try Taza's Almond or Vanilla bar alongside espresso and a sheep's milk cheese, like the Spanish **Ronçal.** Sheep milk's dense fats shine against the acids in coffee, and when you add the sweet surprise of fruit in the chocolate to the hints of cave and nut in the cheese, the combination grows rich and round. If cheese is an indulgence, cheese *and* chocolate is an extravagance, and extravagance is a lovely way to spend an afternoon.

Chocolate and Cheese Throughout the Day

BREAKFAST CHEESE PAIRINGS

Cheeses that might seem unadventurous in the evening prove just right for early daylight hours. Combining them with chocolate's heady zing makes a virtue of their mildness. Try chocolate with fresh chèvre, **Valençay, Piramide di Capra,** and **Bianco di Langa**.

APÉRITIF CHEESE PAIRINGS

Hors d'œuvres, cocktail hour, apéritif, snack, however you name it, this is the moment for venturesome combinations, since our mouths appreciate a bold little bite at sundown: canapés, olives, cured meats, zippy sips of frothy and fermented drinks. Pick interesting cheeses that give the mouth a challenge, then add a few chocolates, and see what mixing and matching them gives: **Taleggio, Reblochon, Ombra, Robiola Castagno.** Every bite may not be a hit, but the experience will be.

DESSERT CHEESE PAIRINGS

Blue cheeses, with their powerful sting of mold and salt, will pair in interesting ways with chocolate at the conclusion of the meal. Since tradition asks you to sweeten the effect of these cheeses with dessert wines or port, let chocolate take that office instead. Nibble your chocolate alongside rich blues like **Stichelton, Persille de Pont Astier, Roquefort Vieux Berger,** and **Fourme d'Ambert**.

OTHER CHOCOLATES TO TRY WITH CHEESE

Dagoba

Dagoba organic chocolate bars, although they certainly fall into the candy category, nevertheless push the chocolate/food boundary, as they include various spices and ingredients culled from the kitchen. The Mint bar yields a savory dose of rosemary, Chai comes with ginger, and other bars feature cherries, oranges, lavender, and black pepper. These culinary hints make Dagoba's bars interesting partners for cheese.

Maglio

If you'd prefer a bar with fewer accessories, Maglio, an Italian chocolate producer, makes beautiful single origin tasting bars from Africa (Tanzania), Cuba, Ecuador, Mexico, Papuasia (Papua New Guinea), Santo Domingo, and Tingo Maria (Peru). In 50-gram packages, the bars offer an easy way to taste the range of flavors unblended cacao can hold: raspberries, tobacco, leather, cherries, apricot, earth. Cheese can hold all these flavors too, so the pairing possibilities are endless. Taste one origin against a range of cheeses or several origins against a single cheese; both approaches will show you just how interesting things get when you mash chocolate and cheese together.

COFFEE

The town of Passenans was waking up when Eric and I arrived in the frost and mist for the *Percée du Vin Jaune*, a yearly festival in the Jura to honor "piercing" new casks of the odd and wonderful oxidized "yellow wine." We, however, were only half awake. Our room at the nearby inn in Poligny was cheerily equipped for *petit déjeuner* with an electric tea kettle, two packets of tea, and a pair of tiny Lavazza espresso cups. How do you make tea in an espresso cup?

An hour later, oddly caffeinated yet still groggy, and definitely hungry, we joined the clusters of French folks wearing wine glasses around their necks and threading the streets of Passenans toward the church, where Mass was being held in honor of the newest vintage of *vin jaune*. Bright marigold pom-poms decked the grey square. We pushed a few steps into the stiflingly crowded church (between heads, I saw a ribboned cask at the foot of the crucifix) and then squeezed back out into the frost to eat.

"Cheese for breakfast," Eric cooed, as though getting away with something. This was before we recognized cheese as a valid breakfast option; in fact, the events of this morning *made* cheese a valid breakfast option. Eric's eyes flitted from vendor to vendor along the narrow main street, where white-capped *fromagers* with red hands began cutting wheels of Comté, Morbier, and Bleu de Gex to fill red-checked paper boats with cheese cubes. I balked. Consuming a pound of cheese before ten (after the preceding day's lunch of cheese, dinner of cheese, and predawn snack of cheese) was beyond me. Eric prevailed, and we ended up sharing the most delicious breakfast we'd ever eaten.

The good news is that to have this breakfast you don't need to be shivering in the drizzling snow at an obscure wine festival. The breakfast starts simply, with a baguette, even a left-over one. Inside the baguette, place a thin slice of *jambon de pays* or Prosciutto di Parma. Then cover the ham with slivers of **Comté (Gruyère** will also do). Heat the whole ensemble lightly. As the heat melts the fat on the ham and the fat in the cheese, it will join them in a translucent blur. This blur oozes into the bread, and the bread crisps against your teeth, and you take another sip of coffee and you're in heaven. Shocking, I know, but the most perfect breakfast in the world is a ham-and-cheese sandwich with black coffee.

The simple combination of coffee and cheese elevates this experience. The bread is a mere foundation, the ham an ornament, and the *Percée du vin jaune*, that February day, was just our scene of discovery. We've pursued the "cheese for breakfast" experiment countless times since and have found that the magic remains even in the simplest coffee and cheese pairing.

For coffee pairs with cheese in a way reminiscent of wine. Just as the acid in wine slices through the fat and cream on your tongue, as if it were breaking apart the individual cheese molecules to inject within them a burst of fruit and mineral, so the acid in coffee slices into cheese's fat, to let you return with new vigor to the cheese. In Arabic, the word "quahwah," from which our English word "coffee" derives, also refers to wine.

Yet coffee has an important characteristic in which it differs from wine. Coffee gets its flavors from the oils in the bean, oils that shift and emerge with roasting. These oils depart from the grounds on contact with hot water, whatever your brewing process. You can often see these oils pooling, iridescent, on the surface of black coffee. Cheese (and *jambon de pays*) also contain oils. When you mingle and heat these treats together, the oils interact. So while the acid in coffee cuts through the cream in cheese, the oils hang back and mingle. Your mouth feels, at once, the sharp sting of acid, the ooze of cheese, and the swirling of mingling oils. On the days when Eric and I enjoy "cheese for breakfast!" this interplay wakes me more than caffeine—or tiny Lavazza espresso cups of tea—ever could.

Cheese for Breakfast!

If you're curious to move beyond the readily recognized breakfast cheeses—cream cheese, cottage cheese, and cheese danish—simply save a bit of whatever cheese you were enjoying the night before and break it out with your morning coffee. The stinkier varieties we have never tried. Better, I think, not to attempt those too close to sunrise.

I can testify that a nice **Robiola Due Latte** or **Robiola Tre Latte** tastes like lark song with apricot preserves; the combo highlights the fruity high notes of a light roast coffee.

The super fatty fat of sheep's milk cheese works well with dark roast coffees, drunk black. A **Brebis Pyrénées** brings out nutty tones. Other sheep's milk cheeses, like **Brebis Pardou** or the Italian **Pecorino di Pienza Monchiato,** can give a grassy warmth to the morning, which might highlight tones of blueberry and earth in the cup.

If you have a hard cheese in the fridge, melt it on some bread for a tastier toast experience than butter can provide. Heating seems to caramelize cheese's flavors, making most cheeses sweeter and easier for morning. **Parmigiano-Reggiano,** a pantry staple, has become a standby toasting cheese at our breakfast table.

Comté, of all cheeses we've tried, makes the happiest

mate for coffee. When you melt it on a baguette, you may well sense the egg that its makers trumpet in its range of possible flavors. Nibbled straight alongside black coffee, the cheese will offer whiffs of cacao and caramel. Comté is a cheese for all hours, not least those earliest hours when, all over the Jura, laitiers like Maurice Etiévant leave their coffee to join the Montbéliardes in the fields.

(AND TEA, TOO)

Should you not be a coffee drinker, don't hesitate to break out your favorite teas with cheese. The flinty, herbal range of green teas harmonizes with the grassy notes in summer cheeses of all milk types, goat, sheep, or cow. Aromatic black teas can heft against the caramel, nut tones in pressed, cooked cheeses. Even a gentle chamomile or *tisane* can coax subtle herbal hues from the milk. Just think, pairing cheese and teas opens up a whole new time for cheese-pairing advenures: High Tea!

FRUIT PRESERVES

Early in our cheese adventures, Eric and I developed rigid ideas about how cheese should be enjoyed. These ideas were meant to respect the integrity of the cheese. We would not, for instance, eat our cheese on bread, since all that carbo mass merely distracted from the cheese, diluting its perfection with starchy blandness. We looked askance at those who spread their Brie, like moldy butter pats, on baguettes. And the cheese plates served in most restaurants, with their heaps of candied pecans and squirts of sweet sauces, seemed shameful. We ate around the accompaniments and dismissed the flavor pairings that the food professionals had crafted and prepared. I say "we," when in fairness, I should perhaps admit that "we" might have been more "me."

My comeuppance came in the kitchen of Vermont cheesemaker Michael Lee. During our visit to Twig Farm, Michael kindly made us lunch at twelve o'clock sharp, as ordained by his progressive countdown, loudly announced to no one in particular, "Lunch in twenty . . . ten . . . five minutes." Gathering the fixings around him on the counter, Michael systematically cut thick slices of whole grain bread. Next he evenly slathered the inside of each slice with dark plum preserves. Then he filled each sandwich with tall slices of his own cheese, the earth-crusted, salt-fleshed **Goat Tomme**. As he pressed the sandwiches in a panini press, I threw Eric an eyebrow raise: He puts *jam* on his *cheese?*

Michael, of course, knew better than I. Instead of distracting from the cheese, as I had feared, the plums highlighted the cheese's best qualities. The abundant flavors of cave and mold on the rind, which might overwhelm the *pâte*, now became a boon: They leant a *gravitas* to the sweetness of the plums. The plums, in turn, sparked youthful and fresh against the grandfatherly depths of the cheese. And balanced between these two poles, between age and youth, between bright and dark, the *pâte* of the cheese sang its hymn of fat and grass and curd and earth. Michael ate three sandwiches. My snobbery was cured. For a brief instant, plum preserves and Twig Farm Goat Tomme married, and it seemed the cosmos swung into a chiming harmony.

Having once tasted harmony, I no longer doubt the pairing of preserves and cheese; I celebrate it. The best pairings I've tasted have struck a balance similar to the one Michael revealed in his plum and Tomme sandwich, a balance between tangy and earthy flavors.

Tangy is the high note, the sharp sweet tone that zips into your sinuses and, occasionally, when sour, makes you salivate from the corners of your jaw. Tangy flavors sometimes have a punchy, bright taste, like a piccolo; sometimes, they're brassy like a trumpet.

Earthy flavors, in contrast, occupy the lower regions of the flavor scale, salty and savory and sometimes even a little bitter: They spread out, all pasture and brine and roast, in your mouth. Earthy flavors sound the baritone and bass notes of the scale, the oboe in its mournful mood, the slow vibrations of a cello.

Now, while I know that Eric doesn't much believe in pairing principles, and while I admittedly risk reverting to a new but equally rigid set of rules about cheese, and while this formula is certainly not foolproof or universally true, here's the principle I've found works for preserves and cheese: Balance tangy and earthy flavors. If you have a goat cheese, for example, that's all tangy citrus and yeasty wheat, you do not want a tangy preserve. So, too, do things get dull when you have too many earth tones at once: Eating brown bread, a moldy rinded cheese, and a mellow preserve will deaden the flavors of all three. In either extreme, tang or earth, the taste buds seem to give up in the face of monotony. Contrast, however, enlivens them, and when you pair contrasting cheese and preserves, they wake up, as if to figure out what's going on.

The best fruit preserves I've ever had come from an Italian farmer, Otello Muccichini. He adds little or no sugar, so the preserves taste more like fruit and less like gummy bears. These preserves are worth tracking down. Once you taste them, you'll want to eat them with a spoon. Simply place a dollop on your plate, or right on the cheese, and experience the enhancing delights of cheese with preserves.

The Principle
for Preserves and Cheese

Earthy cheeses, often aged, have flavors like mushroom, nut, caramel, grass, earth, vegetables, and meat. Enliven them with tangier preserves: raspberry, apricot, cherry, and plum.

Tangy cheeses tend to be younger, to chime with notes of yogurt, citrus, wheat, yeast, fruit, and salt. Mellow them with blueberry, apple, fig, or pear preserves.

PRESERVE AND CHEESE PICKS

A favorite pair: Muccichini's Confettura extra di Albicocche (apricot preserve) and the succulent **Robiola di Capra Carlina** from La Casera di Eros. Some robiolas will be too tangy to marry with apricot preserves. The dense cream of this robiola, with its truffley hues, creates a stellar balance. If you cannot get this particular cheese, a **Robiola Stagionata** or **Roccaverano** should weigh beautifully against the warm, bright apricots.

A second favorite pair: The poire (pear) preserves from Confiture de l'Archèche provide a lovely counterpoint to a young, vibrant goat cheese, like the unpasteurized **Greta's Fairhaven** from Massachusetts' Carlisle Farm. This cheese fits in the palm of your hand and, alongside prevailing bright notes of yogurt and citrus, yields hints of the grass and alfalfa that the goats eat.

Paired with pears, the cheese's sharpness rounds into a delightful, creamy wave.

On the whole, I still prefer preserves with cheeses that offer a clean backdrop against which the preserves can dance. So, for instance, I would not put preserves on Comté, as that cheese already has a whole array of fruit and other flavors happening within it. But the nicely spiced Italian **Caprotto,** the pure Belgian **Charmoix** and **Wavreumont,** or the mild French **Mille Trous** will each work with a wide array of preserves.

You might try the adventure of tasting several preserves with each of these cheeses, to see how they influence the flavors in the cheese. A nice way to experience that is through the preserve sampler from Les Confitures Raphaël, an organic producer in Brittany. The sampler's adorable two-ounce jars couldn't be cheerier, and along with the familiar preserve flavors—cherry, blueberry, strawberry, orange, and so forth—some surprising flavors creep in—kiwi, grapefruit, rhubarb. There's even a *confit d'oignon*. I admit you might need to try that last one on some bread.

HONEY

I pulled out my 1872 edition of *The Language of Flowers: An Alphabet of Floral Emblems* to see what secret messages the honey flowers, ones that bees frequent, might express. The Victorians took a practice that had been around since the Middle Ages—using flowers to send messages—and codified it in small guides to floriography. Indexed by both "Flowers, and the Sentiments Which They Represent" and "Sentiments, and the Flowers Which Represent Them," my slim volume would ensure that a giver or receiver of flowers could decipher the exact message a bouquet contained. I turned to the honey flowers. From the chestnut's plea, "Do me justice," to the clover's urging for "Industry," from the buzz kill of the rhododendron's warning, "Danger," to sage's praise of "Domestic virtues," honey flowers yield a disappointing set of messages. Of the lot, only the dandelion, "Love's oracle," could inspire a fluttering fan or dropped handkerchief.

Still, honey's aura of romance remains. A field of wild flowers gets distilled into a golden haze in a glass jar. The sun, the wind and waving grass, poems by Keats and paintings by Dante Gabriel Rossetti, all captured and contained on my spoon. It's magic. If you've ever tested the allure of edible flowers, you've likely learned that flowers are hardly edible according to everyday standards of taste. Dry and starchy, a dandelion is *not* good eating. But in dandelion honey, there is spring, preserved through winter's snows, in golden hues and warm smells. The magic of honey is that when you eat it, you eat—without actually having to eat them—flowers.

Or so I thought. Let me undeceive you as I have been undeceived: Honey is bee vomit. Yes, bee vomit.

For the flowers, I had almost reconciled myself to bees' presence in the honey process. (Encountered in life, bees make me scream.) I had studiously avoided all thoughts of the hive, with its nightmarish science-fiction world of insect drones making combs and fanning larvae. I had repressed, by sheer force of will, the memory of Eric's "Hey, come look at this," when he'd keyed "Bee beard" into a Google image search. All this trauma I had overcome, for the honey, for the flowers.

However, if honey tangentially comes from flowers, it more nearly comes from bees. And it turns out that bees—while revoltingly terrifying—are also incredible creatures. Even a cursory look at what bees do astonishes. They can release pheromones to mark spots particularly rich in nectar or navigate to their hive. They can secrete from their heads a royal jelly that, when given in higher quantity to some larvae, transforms them into queens and, when consumed by humans, is touted to do everything from prevent aging to cure disease. And bees have queens, for God's sake, one in every sixty thousand who commands the hive. If all this were not enough, bees also make honey in a process so astonishing it almost outweighs how gross it is that when you eat honey you are eating bee vomit.

See, bees bring flower nectar back to the hive in their honey stomachs, then regurgitate it into the mouths of other bees. These bees then regurgitate and reswallow it several times, adding enzymes to partially digest it. When it reaches the proper consistency, they place it (puke it) into the honeycombs.

More bees fan the combed honey with their wings, to increase the evaporation of water and prevent fermentation, before it's capped with wax and stored for future food needs. Then we swoop in, pure pirates, and steal the nectar the bees have painstakingly preserved to help them survive the winter months.

Honey can also help caseophiles survive winter months. Winter cheeses often taste like a skim milk variety of their spring and summer counterparts, sickly and pale, dull in the comparison. The reason for this difference lies partly in what the animals are—or rather aren't—eating. In winter, they subsist on dry feed: in the best cases, grasses threshed straight from the pastures where the animals graze; in the worst cases, industrial grains and feeds. What's missing in both cases is the flowers, the dandelions that, in April, make the milk bright yellow, the clover and violets that add perfume throughout the summer. Even a cheese as sturdy as Cheddar transforms when the herds move to the fields in bloom. Eric and I once tasted a **Montgomery Farmhouse Cheddar** so grassy, so herbaceously bloomy, so *green*, we kept gasping. I wanted to recite Marvell's Mower poems: "Where willing Nature does to all dispense / A wild and fragrant innocence." It was as if the cheesemakers had hidden salad inside the cheese. The green and floral flavors in cheeses are usually more nuanced than that, but when those nuances disappear, much of the beauty and surprise of a cheese disappear too.

Honey can bring them back again. When you eat honey with your cheese, sparks of the spring and summer pastures return. You taste clovers, dandelions, lavender, and wild flowers, budding again, fragrant again, preserved (by way of many bee stomachs) and glowing on your spoon.

Cheese and Bee Vomit

Honey tastes best with goat's milk cheeses, young and tangy ones. It may be that the mouth is already primed to taste flowers there, since in spring milk, unpasteurized goat cheeses, it will. Happily, honey goes a long way toward filling the flavor gap that occurs in winter and pasteurized versions of French and Italian small-format goat cheeses. Pasteurization, after all, kills the flavor-making bacteria that carry *terroir* and blossom into the cheese. Wonderful cheeses like **Sainte-Maure, Valençay, Charollais, Sancerre, and Tarentais,** which feel dull in their pasteurized American incarnations, wake up with a bit of honey. The Italian goat cheeses, **Piramide di Capra** and **Sigarot di Capra** or **Sigarot alla Cenere,** do too. Even a cheese vibrant on its own, like the washed **Tomme de Chèvre au Muscadet** reveals interesting new notes from the addition of honey.

A meaty honey, like the opaque, butterscotch-colored Montagne from Lo Brusc in Provence will match with weightier cheeses. This honey has an animal heft, as if the bees were sipping nectar in the barnyard. Its dark, savory quality will need a sturdy, sweet cheese to balance it. Try **Brebis Ossau, Salers,** or **Raclette,** which, like the honey, come from high mountain elevations.

The liveliest, most incredible honey I've ever tasted comes from an Italian producer in Piedmont, Floriano Turco. His honeys have a tropical-looking bird on the label and taste insanely lush. A tiny spoonful sends a jolt of delight straight through my being. I love the acacia honey, which has a hint of pine resin to it, and the rhododendron, which roughs up your tongue with coarse crystals, only to soothe it with a creamy, delicate afterglow. It tastes intensely *floral*, even for a honey. Sip it when you think you cannot stand another day of gray skies, another month of rain.

If this honey is still not cheer enough, you might try one of Floriano's honeys alongside the beautiful Italian cheese **Candela delle Langhe**. It comes coated in yellow beeswax with blossoms pressed into the top. Candela delle Langhe is like a posy for your mouth; with Floriano's honey, it's poetry.

MEAT

—

"Sometimes, I'd rather *not* know where my food comes from, you know?" I looked around the kitchen at Twig Farm, seeking an amen. Eric crinkled his brow beseechingly, as he does when I, accidentally and with the best of intentions, wish a Jewish person "Merry Christmas." Emily, who runs the business side of the farm, turned away with a blank smile, suddenly fascinated by the refrigerator. Michael Lee, cheesemaker and goatherd, eyed me with disbelief.

Michael and Emily not only raise their own goats to make cheese, but also can point to each neighboring farm that raises the cows, chickens, and pigs they eat. They value knowing what journey an animal or vegetable has taken to become food on their plates. They face this process on their own farm every year, when they must send off their male kids (since they cannot produce milk) to become dinners for someone else. "You don't have a name," Michael informed one spotted kid unlucky to have been born male. Michael's farm *is* where food comes from.

My comment made me the enemy, the oafish fast-food eater who embodies mindless consumption. "Come on," I seemed to be saying, "let the cows live in filth and misery in industrial complexes where people in hazmat suits pump them full of steroids and antibiotics, and then, after miserable sunless lives, subject them to painful, panicked deaths. And once that irritating, live animal part is over with, please process the meat into oblivion, rounding out the questionable quantities of gristle and bone and organ and offal with artificial 'meat' flavors, so that the 'meat' tastes reassuringly uniform and unspecific to any place or season or breed. Then go ahead and ship this 'meat' all over the world, adding pollution and oil dependence and the destruction of small farms like yours, Michael, to the pleasure of the unconscionable, unhealthy, and unidentifiable 'meat' I so enjoy. Long live fast food. Death to Twig Farm."

What I'd *meant* to express was merely my vexed relationship to meat. Most days, I am a practical, if not ideological, vegetarian. Beef tongues, encountered even across the safe distance of a deli case, make me queasy. Egg yolks are a distinct challenge. I'd rather not find bones on my dinner plate; then again, the vague textures inside a sausage distress me. There was a moment in France when the presence of an unexpected kidney in my salad made me cry. What I was attempting to express at Twig Farm, when I offended our hosts, was that while, of course, I want the meat I eat when I do eat meat to come from animals that are well treated, healthily fed, and humanely killed, I can enjoy meat only when it's somewhat abstracted from its point of origin, the animal it once was and now isn't anymore.

Perhaps this ambivalence explains why the meats I most enjoy taste like something else. Jamón Ibérico de Bellota offers the supreme instance of this meat amnesia. It's cured pork, yes, and it has all the characteristics of cured pork: a saltiness, a sweetness, a swirling surface that mimics, in rose flesh and white fat, the constellations and cloud shapes of Van Gogh's skies. This jamón also costs about as much as one of Van Gogh's paintings, so it's good that a tiny bite can be transporting. It smells like toasted autumn. When you place the jamón on a warmed plate, as you should, the texture shifts, and the fat becomes translucent, as if sunlight were melting through those clouds. And when you finally taste it, almost nervous with anticipated delight, the flavor seeps into your tongue and your eyes widen in wonder.

Later, you may remember the incredible story of black pigs who roam wooded pastures and eat only acorns, for you'll taste the acorns in the meat. But this story will fade, because the animal the meat once was will seem a sublime and mythical creature who lived a sublime and mythical life, nourished on sublime and mythical foods unknown to humans until now, but which you consume through the jamón. You wait with it in your mouth, stilled before some power, almost afraid to move or breathe, certainly unwilling to swallow. But then, as Emily Dickinson tells it, "True Poems flee—" and the flavor is gone before you can grasp it. You catch your breath and lift another sublime and mythical fragment to your lips.

I'm not exaggerating. Okay, I'm exaggerating, but still, you must try it. Crazy as the cost is (almost two hundred dollars per pound), a slice or two of jamón costs only as much as a movie ticket. And how often can you taste, for the price of a movie ticket, the most sublime, expensive, transporting instance of a given food in the world? Taste Jamón Ibérico with firelight or candlelight, a beloved companion, a full-mouthed wine, and a subtle cheese to highlight the jamón's nutty, vegetal notes. The sheep's milk cheese, **U Pecurinu,** from Corsica, is an obliging partner, complementary without competing. Then again, what could compete?

Meats That Pair Well
with Cheese

Clearly, every day cannot be a Jamón Ibérico day, so let me suggest a few other meats that will allow you to forget, a bit more frequently, that you're eating meat.

BRESAOLA

Bresaola is an air-cured beef that often has a terrifying greenish hue to it. "Is it rotting?" you'll wonder. It may be. I once heard a monger say it tastes "like sucking on rusty nails." In case these descriptors do not lure you, let me add that it's dry and primal, meat freed from the frills and fussiness of cuisine. We're not talking beef jerky here, the American West and cowboy fires and sweaty leather; no, bresaola is Old World, unpretentious yet elegant, how I imagine meat might taste at a marriage feast in one of Mozart's lighter operas. You pull at it with your teeth, and it pulls back, but not enough to muss your hair. Try it with a cheese not unlike Mozart's own reputed personality, irascible and brilliant. A semi-soft, washed rind would do well, say a younger **Taleggio** or even Twig Farm's own **Washed Wheel** cheese. The moist smack of the cheese *pâte* will draw out the meat's hidden juices.

PROSCIUTTO DI PARMA

Prosciutto di Parma and **Parmigiano-Reggiano** are such a natural pairing that I'm almost embarrassed to mention them, in case it sounds like I think I am reinventing the wheel or rediscovering gravity. I'm not. I commend this obvious pairing simply because it's so ideal. The pigs drink the whey produced in making Parmigiano-Reggiano, so the meat already tastes like Parmigiano-Reggiano. Less obviously, tasting the two together lets you taste notes of meat in the cheese. Like the best pairings, this one not only highlights the strengths in each element, it also corrects their weaknesses. And to be honest, Parmigiano-Reggiano—however much the Italians tout it as the "King of Cheese"—strikes me as a bit crusty and humorless when eaten on its own, more maiden aunt than king. So too, for all the delights of our favorite variety of prosciutto, Prosciutto di Parma Pio Tosini, Eric rightly observes that it can taste overly perfumey, like walking past a lady who's hosed it on too thick. But when you pair the perfume of Prosciutto Pio Tosini with the sweet dryness of **Parmigiano-Reggiano Cravero**'s fruity notes, or with the surprising cinnamon kick of a **Parmigiano-Reggiano Riserva,** the result is neither perfumed nor dry. It's lush and savory and rich. As we tasted the meat and cheeses together, I tried to express the explosiveness of the combination and failed. Eric placed the two together on a bit of bread, chewed, grinned, and sighed, "I could eat that a lot and be happy."

SALAME TOSCANO FINOCCHIONA

The Italian Salame Toscano Finocchiona is fat-speckled and vibrant with spices. It zips into your mouth like a shiny fennel bicycle, bright metal all aglow. This meat needs a sturdy cheese, like the adventurously molded **Crosta di Pane,** to stand up to its fennel-laden zing. Or, if you wish to make the salame the main event, then choose a more delicate cheese, like the Italian goat's milk **Sigarot di Capra Naturale,** to cleanse your palate with its simplicity, so you can return ready for the Fioncchiona's bright energy.

NIMAN RANCH HAM or BERKSHIRE HERITAGE HAM

These hams are straightforward and fragrant. Choose them when you have a diva cheese that demands all the attention. Or choose them when you really want a chop or steak sort of meat experience, since, even sliced thin, they retain a juiciness that makes the mouth salivate. Their simple, luscious character pleases alongside the oozing glow of a **Robiola** beginning to run.

OLIVES

Until a few years ago I thought olives came in two kinds: black and green. Black olives were the treat of childhood holidays and company visits, gorged in handfuls by my brothers and me. Salty and rubbery, they squeaked happily when we chewed them. Green olives, served only at my grandparents' house, always seemed vaguely militaristic, their color that of a dusty wool uniform, and that inexplicable pimento a flag or feather in its peaked cap. I once made the mistake of tasting one. It was sour and, compared with its black counterpart, a nightmarish fraud.

Both olives came from the can, pitted and awash in salty liquor. Both seemed unidentifiable with any natural origin. They revealed two texture options, squishy and squeaky. And the flavor palate never wavered from sour and salty. For the longest time, I wondered at, and couldn't answer, my own question: What *are* olives? Vegetables? Nuts? Candy?

Only when I encountered olives as an adult did I realize that olives are a *fruit*. An olive bar looks like a miniature fruit stand: Crimson as cherries, purple as plums, the orange of apricots, olives are not dusty like the green olives I had loathed, but vibrant and alive. Swimming in their brine and oil baths, they become a natural element, as saturated as the multicolored pebbles in the bottom of a stream. The stones in the olives' centers—I never even knew olives had stones—further reveal the olive's fruity nature. Cherries, after all, have pits. Plums and apricots too.

The pit is much more than an obstacle to be gotten past. It's an opportunity. For in the adherence of flesh to pit, and the varied ratio between the two, olives transcend the squeaky-squishy range of textures found in pitted olives or those, like I knew, from a can. Some olives surrender their pit no more easily than a peach. The taut meat of the shiny green Lucques from Languedoc forces you to scrape and suck for every scrap of flesh. Lucques comes off its pit in shards. The raisined skins of Nyons, with the earthy hues of organs, appear slightly deflated. Poking in on all sides, Nyons look bruised in the bowl, and the pit slips between the collapsing folds with the barest hint of pressure.

Today I would choose one green olive over all the options arrayed in the vastest bars: Castelvetrano. The name sounds magical; it conjures up crenellated castles and forests with primeval ferns. Yet in appearance, Castelvetrano olives look clean and fresh. Pulling one from the bowl, you go bobbing in a barrel of tiny Granny Smith apples. The pleasure of Castelvetrano lies in their malleability. Picked young in southern Sicily and cured in salt brine rather than vinegar, they retain a sweetness and mildness that other olives lose in the journey from tree to table. As you crunch them (and they really do crunch), the olive hints at sweet buttered bread and fresh grass in the sunshine.

This clean palate offers the ideal backdrop for other, less simple flavors. Add a glass of opulent Verdicchio; it will highlight the olive's lush green tone. The two textures seem to call out the abundance in each other: As you sip and chew, you'll feel the olive spread out in oily waves against your teeth. The light cherry flavors of a Dolcetto d'Alba will lift with fruity sweetness, while the olive replies with a satisfying nip of salt. A more tannic red, like Saumur, will pare the olive down, bringing its bite to the back of your tongue. Instead of grass, you'll taste earth, a hint of bitterness that nicely moderates the Castelvetrano's buttery sweetness.

Pits, Rinds, and Wine: Pairing Olives and Cheese

Olives—even beyond the canned pimento-decked greens of youth—can have a sourness, both from the fruit and the brine. This sourness makes pairing olives a challenge, for once the briny taste of vinegar strikes the tongue, it can season even delightful wines with hues of vinegar. Adding cheese to the mix can temper that sourness and allow the three companions to complement each other.

CASTELVETRANO

Castelvetrano olives mix especially well with sheep's milk cheese. A perfect picnic spread: Castelvetrano, Marcona almonds, and **Bra Duro** or a young Pecorino (like **Pecorino Cafone**). As you move between them, the flavors build together in your mouth. Soon, you're tasting cream in the olives, green olive in the almonds, and nut in the cheese. Even if you're picnicking in your kitchen, you'll feel across all three the salty brush of sea air against a sunny hill.

LUCQUES

Lucques, like Castelvetrano, have firm, green flesh. But where Castelvetrano olives hum with buttery plushness,

Lucques have more pinch about them. You might catch hints of herbaceous bitters as you chew. For balance, pair these olives with a bright lemony cheese, like the youthful **Pecorino Paglierino**.

NYONS

Cured in olive oil and salt, Nyons have a delicious range of textures and colors. The bowl wobbles with shades of purple: purple plum, mustard purple, inky purple, iron-red purple and purply brown. With their deep flavor, Nyons taste like something that should burrow in the ground. Cheese again offers a chance for levity. A **Garrotxa** pairs the brightness of goat's milk with some earthy hues of its own, so it makes a pleasing match for the earthen Nyons. A fully bright cheese, like the Spanish **Leonora,** will also lighten the penumbra Nyons create in your mouth.

OLIVE OIL–CURED BLACK OLIVES
WITH *HERBES DE PROVENCE*

I still want to eat black olives by the handful. I have, however, left the rubberized canned variety behind, to appreciate the balance of herbs and fruit that these olives offer. You'll want to lick off the dried herbs that cling to your fingertips, so eat them among friends. Try them with a quality Gouda-style cheese, like **Reypenaer V.S.O.P.** (the cheese's protein crystals create a nice texture parallel to herb-flecked olives). An Alpine cheese will also round out the olives with a nutty sweetness. **Appenzeller** keeps hints of grass that you and the herbed olives will enjoy.

WHISKEY

Homicide detective James Hennigan is the type of man I thought existed only in stories by Raymond Chandler, Cormac McCarthy, Ernest Hemingway: A taciturn, Irish, hard-drinking war vet, he works cases in Chicago's grittiest neighborhood, the south side. Graveyard is not just the shift, but the destination, and August is a murder jubilee. Once a year, he ventures to Cambridge to guest-teach a class on observation to Eric's "kiddos" (as Hennigan calls the Harvard undergrads) and presents a slide show of crime scenes. Every year, a student faints. Jim is the one who has schooled us in whiskey.

The first lesson was the familiar kind: You try to keep up with a man's man who drinks "the brown stuff" like water and then, five hours later, drives you home with steady hands, while you, throughout a sleepless night of spinning floors and between trembles the next morning, swear never to touch that stuff again.

Over the years, subsequent lessons have been kinder, and Jim has introduced us to our favorite whiskeys. Without Jim, we'd never have ventured beyond the well-known Jack's, Jim's, and Grandad's (a bourbon that he tells us is not whiskey at all) and, because of Jim, we've still never ventured into Scotch (the mention of it occasions sneers from the Irish in him). While he swears to liking whiskey only for its effect—"Who gives a crap what it tastes like?"—his recommendations have never tasted like crap. In fact, they always have a distinctly refined edge to them, which he, of course, denies.

When we approached him, as we do in all whiskey-related matters, for advice about pairing whiskey with cheese, Jim's mustached lip curled. In principle, he doesn't believe in having food and booze together ("What's the point?"), least of all whiskey and "curdled fermented bovine ovine effluence." So, with him insisting, "I don't know my ass from my gruyère," Eric and I realized that we were on our own.

Pairing whiskey and cheese requires the kind of strategic imagination involved in pitting prizefighters against each other or staging maneuvers for armies. We realized this challenge at a tasting of American whiskey and farmstead cheese that we attended at New York's Astor Center. The evening's host, Ethan Kelley of the Brandy Library, consistently spoke of the pairings in bellicose terms: The whiskey was "killing" the cheese, or the cheese was "wrestling" with the whiskey. Kelley admitted to priding himself on not seeking pairings that worked, so much as pairings that were interesting, even if that meant they "clashed," "fought," and "did battle" in your mouth.

In this battle, most of the cheeses picked by Toni Amira, Artisanal's Director of Sales, simply didn't stand a chance. A New York triple crème called **Nettle Meadow Kunik** became, in Eric's words, little more than "butter with a crust" against the vanilla, wood-fisted punch of the Kansas whiskey, Most Wanted. Or take the **Laurier,** a fresh goat's milk cheese from Vermont, wrapped in bay leaves: It's one of the best-selling cheeses at Artisanal, no doubt because of the delightful nuances the fresh bay infuses into the clean milk. Yet, against the big malt flavors of the night—Canadian Club Sherry Cask, Saint George Single Malt (which could slay dragons), and Buffalo Trace Straight Bourbon (think Wild West)—that delicacy became a mere suggestion of fat on the tongue. On the whole, the pairings tended more toward confrontation than conversation, and the whiskey shouted louder.

At the moment when we were beginning to worry that maybe Jim was right to eschew dairy "effluence" with brown booze, a winning pair pointed the way to success: **Tarentaise,** an Alpine style cheese from Vermont, faced off with Corner Creek Reserve Bourbon. The cheese, made in the style of the French Abondance, won the American Cheese Society's "Best Farmstead Cow's Milk Cheese" award and, from its cocky strut across my tongue, Tarentaise seemed to know it was all that. Kelley called the bourbon something of a "baby Bourbon," and I could see why, since it was still swaddled in the natural flavors of grain and herbs. "I've got a flower right here on the tip of my nose," Toni Amira marveled as he sniffed it. Eric drew a more colorful analogy: "It's what Harry Potter's school blazer would smell like after a summer afternoon in the woods with that big giant." When we put the grassy youth of the bourbon and the prize-winning maturity of the cheese together, they seemed less like rivals than rollicking siblings. Floral notes bounced back and forth. The kick of the whiskey sunk into the cooked cream of the cheese, and then the whiskey smiled as the cheese kicked back. This was a pairing of well-matched adversaries, maybe even, by the end of the night, comrades.

Whiskey and Cheese Strategies

Bring a strategic mind to pairing whiskey and cheese, as you'll need to weigh them strength for strength. In fact, harmonious pairings will probably bring a gentler whiskey up against a strong cheese.

CHEESE-READY WHISKEYS

Pick whiskeys that retain something of the field about them. Those with strong vanilla, pine, fire, butterscotch, smoke, and peat flavors tend to carry more punch than the majority of cheeses can handle. An herbaceous booze, however, will shine against the grassy notes many cheeses carry. Those refined whiskeys Jim would not deign to pair with cheeses actually tasted quite good with them.

Knappogue Castle 1994

The 1994 Knappogue is light and crisp and fresh. Those are words more often used of white wine than whiskey and they suggest precisely the character that allows this whiskey to pair well with cheese. There's a distinctive suggestion of well water here, rich minerals, and an almost refreshing clarity. Instead of eradicating the subtle flavors of cheeses, like the delicate pineapple in **Berkswell** or the nuts in **Vermont Dandy,** Knappogue coaxes them into conversation with its own subtle notes of citrus and fresh fruit.

Tyrconnell Irish Whiskey

Tyrconnell also makes a merit of its delicacy when you pair it with cheese. Some hints of flora arrive in the nose, then you get the bright crisp of apples on your tongue. The apple flavor sings with the Calvados-washed Normandy cheese, **Grain d'Orge.** But a washed rind is not the only option: This is a whiskey that remains open to influences from whatever cheese you select. A cheese with flavors of nut and caramel, like the French Pyrénées' **Istara,** will coax out spices in the whiskey. A grassier, vegetal cheese, like **Bergkase Bio Berghoff** or the Swiss **Senne Flada,** will pull out from the whiskey the tang of orange and the dusk of malt.

Baker's Bourbon, 7 year

From the wheaty shades of Knappogue and Tyrconnell we come to the deep hazelnut of Baker's, and the color alone reveals that this is a meatier drink. For all the rich sweetness of caramel, cinnamon, and vanilla in the smell, Baker's also remains smooth and light in the mouth. This levity gives cheese a chance. Cheeses with notes of caramel and caramelized nuts, like **Boerenkaas-Veenweidekaas** from the Netherlands, will balloon the bourbon's flavor as the fat coats your mouth, and then the mingled sweet notes of the cheese, carried on the bourbon's vapors, will reach deep into your brain.

WHISKEY-READY CHEESES

The light, clear whiskeys I've named will let more delicate cheeses stand on their own beside them. Sometimes you want a cheese than can hold its own against the strongest flavors, against a rasping Bourbon, a peaty Scotch (though Jim proposes that the best match for Scotch is likely "dead Tudor"). Here are some cheeses you can nibble alongside pitchers of gasoline, ammonia, vinegar, and compost, and still taste the cheese.

Ardrahan

I made a histrionic note in our cheese journal, "God save us." Whiskey alone can save this cheese, and whiskey saves it so well, it becomes tangy and alive.

Fiocco del Bec

This goat cheese from Piedmont is like eating an entire goat. A monger described it to us as "hoofy," and that word really captures the experience: a bit of foot and farmyard, the ooze of slime, the redolence of poo. It's alluring and disgusting at the same time. You cringe and yet take another bite. With whiskey, this cheese's stink fades into the background, leaving a pleasant animal smell, like the scent that clings to you after an afternoon on horseback.

Morbier

A grouchy old man of a cheese, Morbier is crotchety, smelly, and bitter. Like any worthy curmudgeon, Morbier wrinkles its wrinkled brow at the newfangled ways of youth, since its makers continue the age-old tradition of separating the morning and evening milk with a layer of vegetable ash. That ash pulls smoky, ashen notes from whiskey. A whiskey with some sweetness—an Annie of a whiskey—will sweeten Morbier's somewhat codgery disposition.

Livarot

Ah, the little Colonel, the bog monster, cheese of the weeping sinuses. We tasted a punishing Livarot in Paris, and the memory still stings. But Livarot need not be a punishment. Eaten at its prime, Livarot can be charmingly pungent and earthen. Its (ahem) fragrances will please most against an equally staunch booze.

WINE

I like to think I'm not alone in wishing, every once in a while, to have a universal ticket book to cite those who break the rules. Have we not all been victim of one or more of the common daily criminals: those who honk when no honking is needed, those who neglect to de-ice the sidewalk, droppers and leavers of fruit in the grocery store, rude salespeople who snap for no reason. I once found a ticket book on the hood of a station wagon, left there, it seems, by a preoccupied traffic cop. What a dilemma: If I took it, I could enforce the rules, but if I took it, I would break the rules.

Outlining rules for pairing wine and cheese might seem to satisfy in me the occasional rule-enforcing desire, since this pairing, above all others, tends to inspire strict rules. Yet, in this case, I feel more comfortable on the side of outlaw than lawman. In fact, any time I try to wrangle my own wine experiences into rules, I hear the throaty scorn of a hypothetical wine aficionado who inhabits my inferiority complex. He wears a 1920s tuxedo and speaks with an Evelyn Waugh-esque accent: "And cahn you believe it? She thought to serve cheeses from the Loire with a red from Burgundy! Mwah hahaha haa. Doesn't she know that cheeses from the Loire must look south for pairings, as the sun does across the vineyards along the Cher in summah." Look into wine pairing and you'll find that sort of guy, ready to direct you with rules.

Even someone like Steven Jenkins, who opens his admirable *Cheese Primer* with the friendly reassurance, "Choosing wine to serve with cheese is not something you need to get all worked up about," closes the book by detailing "Appropriate Wines" to serve with each of the "Great Cheeses" he praises. It's laudable that Jenkins avoids normative terms like "best" or "ideal" in favor of that more mellow adjective, "appropriate." This word indeed makes his choices feel less like rules and more like invitations. And yet, that word brings negative associations to my ear. Choosing an "inappropriate" wine, one not included on the "appropriate" list, would seem to class one linguistically with those who shout lewd remarks in "inappropriate" settings or make "inappropriate" advances on a first date. Spinning this term in the most positive direction, it still feels a little damning: To hear someone say, "Ah, yes, this wine is appropriate," would not feel like praise of your pairing.

Ideally, I'd like for us all to be able to venture into wine and cheese pairing without fear of breaking the rules or descending into inappropriateness. Yet even mongers whose talents I hold in the highest esteem sometimes get a bit tense around the eyes when I face them with the question: "What wine would you pair with this cheese?"

Freedom for me came in that familiar saying that bread, wine, and cheese are the Holy Trinity of the French table. Intended as a witticism, the theological analogy actually suggests to me something true about the experience of pairing wines with cheese and bread: It's a matter of belief. Christian theologians since the fourth century have devised rules and weighed in with terms like "perichorisis" and "hypostasis" to parse the precise way that the Trinity is made up of Father,

Son, and Spirit, three persons, one God. Yet the Trinity
remains, for all their efforts, a mystery that only faith ulti-
mately can affirm. Wine experts, in their turn, have waxed on
with rules and systems, have debated *terroir*, varietals, residual
sugars, and weather patterns to parse how wine, cheese, and
bread best come together into one flavor that transcends the
individual parts. Yet this, too, is a matter of faith, and tasting
alone is often the basis for conversion: Like Paul on the road
to Damascus, you're blinded by a sudden flash of brilliance on
your tongue and you suddenly, unequivocally believe that the
Loire goat cheese, Sancerre, and a glass of Sancerre, when
paired together, make heaven.

If, however, you merely read an expert's recommendation that you should drink Sauvignon Blanc with a Loire goat
cheese you've never tasted (and can get only in pasteurized
form in the United States), that suggestion is unlikely to
convince you that the pairing is transcendent, particularly if
you know already that you do not like Sauvignon Blanc or
if you generally prefer whites from Germany. Nor will that
recommendation likely convince you to seek out a Sauvignon Blanc, particularly if the bottle the expert recommends
costs even ten dollars more than your standard price. I, for
instance, know I hate Riesling. I have been to five different
Riesling-centered tastings, where I've tasted fine bottles from
worthy vineyards, yet I will never choose to drink a bottle of
Riesling, no matter who recommends it or with what cheese
it promises to be divine. When it comes to Riesling, I am
simply not a believer.

So, the best wine pairing guideline I could offer, here in
my final Chuck's pick, is to play with what you know you

love. Start with a wine you already believe in and play around to see what cheeses make it live a better, fuller life in your mouth.

The most transcendent pairings I've enjoyed have come from watching the wines I already love light up in unexpected ways from the sudden interjection of a cheese's personality. Just the other night, Eric and I got woozy with delight when (because we had both in the house) we paired a Chardonnay from the Jura with a Belgian cheese made in the style of the Touraine goat cheese, **Sainte-Maure**. This cheese has no real parallel in the cheese styles of the Jura, the kind that would naturally complement that wine. And a Jura Chardonnay is a far cry from the range of wines experts recommend to complement the Sainte-Maure: Vouvray (made from the grape Chenin Blanc), Bourgogne-Aligoté (Aligoté), and Muscadet (Melon de Bourgogne) all tend to be more acidic, salty even, with strong minerals, and full to the brim with crisp bright fruit. And yet, oh, how the warm floral spice in the wine pooled into the limestony cream of the cheese, and how they flew off in my mouth to make a heaven where flavor profiles and geographical borders do not exist.

This is what the best wine and cheese pairings do: They transform the individual elements into something more than each could be alone. Am I quoting Eric? He said something like this when he talked about Sancho Panza and Don Q, how pairing is comedy. I might draw an analogy to what theologians say happens in the Eucharist, how bread and wine become Christ's mystical body and blood. You put two ordinary things together, and, suddenly, though you cannot explain how, you get transcendence.

Perhaps the best analogy for pairings does not come from religion or literature, but rather from romance, because choosing pairings is like matchmaking. You taste the unique character of a cheese, then scroll through the wines you know and enjoy, calling their flavors into your mind. As you do, you place that cheese and each wine in conversation: Would they be interesting together? Would they spark? Do they share common notes? Would there be chemistry? Sometimes, as on blind dates, it clicks, and you get a match.

As anyone who has fallen in love or watched someone fall in love knows, there are no rules to romance. Jane Austen's matchmaking heroine, Emma, learned this truth when she tried to pair her lowly friend Harriet with the snobby Mr. Elton. He was a perfect match for her, according to Emma's misguided sense of matchmaking. But Emma didn't account for just how horrid matches can be when they follow rules instead of romance. Happily, Harriet breaks away from Emma's matchmaking and marries the man whom Emma thought all wrong, yet was Harriet's true match from the start, the farmer, Robert Martin. So, too, I think the best pairings in cheese and wine are not those dictated by rules, but those that broaden and deepen our pleasure in that which we already love.

This understanding dawned on me the other night, as Eric and I sipped our Jura Chardonnay alongside that gorgeous Sainte-Maure from Belgium. Eric grinned and said of the pairing, "These two are having a really good first date." And I thought, "No question, it's love."

Wines I Love
and the Cheeses That Love Them

Although I've decried the power of pairing recommendations, I can't resist naming here some wines I wholly believe in, along with the cheeses they seem most to cherish.

SPARKLING

It turns out that when winemakers *don't* wallop their sparkling wines with sugar syrup (and most *do*), the wines actually sparkle more as still wines do, with bursts of fruit, flower, and rock. Since this discovery, Eric and my favorite bubbly wines are *"nondosé"* or low in "dosage." These less-sweetened wines prove more cheese friendly than more doséd ones, as they have more character of their own to bring to the match.

Pierre Gimonnet, Blanc des Blancs Brut Premier Cru & Langres

This low dosage *blanc des blancs* sparkles like silver trout scales glimpsed through the ripples of the coldest, clearest stream. Despite this rustic analogy, the wine tastes less of nature than civilized opulence. My first sip dispersed the long-standing jealousies I'd suffered since reading *Brideshead Revisited*, where Sebastian and Charles Rider soak all summer in fine champagnes. This wine tastes exactly how I'd always imagined that gorgeous, Old World, moneyed family champagne would. In whatever context you sip it, its elegance will make you feel as if you're drinking it from crystal. When it streaks through the fleshy *pâte* of a Langres, you'll admire its strength as well as its delicacy.

Château Tour Grise, Brut Non Dosé & Selles-sur-Cher

A sparkling Saumur from the Loire, this wine is mischievous. As you pop the cork, your mouth gets revved for the habitual frills of sparkling wine, but on the first sip, you encounter instead an almost austere quietude. Imagine entering a gallery expecting to see Renoir's children and finding Whistler's seascapes hanging there: Instead of exuberance, you get meditation; instead of pastels, you gaze at earth tones. "Tour Grise," literally "Gray Tower," seems a fitting name for this wine, since it towers in the mouth with hints of gray rock and sandy beaches. The wine's mineralities make it a delicious match for an ash-covered cheese, like Selles-sur-Cher. I'd serve the pair with fresh fruit on the side, to coax the wine's fruit into brightness.

WHITE

Eric and I tend to go in for whites that are richly textured, that roll around in the mouth with lush, plush fullness. We especially dig wines that have the odd savory hint to their flavor, like Bourgogne-Aligoté's saline quality or the delightful onion-and-garlic resonances in some Sancerre. These characteristics interact in interesting ways with the savory tones of cheese.

Stéphane Tissot, Savagnin (2004)
& Marcel Petite's Comté le Fort

Savagnin is our favorite grape from our favorite region, the Jura. When aged *sous-voile*, under a film of yeast, Savagnin becomes the magnificent *vin jaune* we'd savored in the Jura. Before we'd tasted *vin jaune*, David, a monger at Formaggio, warned us, "It smells like the musty basement of some- one with lots of cats." Now, I can see why he would say that. On the nose, there *is* a whiff of city in summer, but the taste is so much richer and more sumptuous than that smell would lead you to expect, that the fragrance too, in retrospect, becomes a part of the experience's rich sur- prise. Savagnin wines share *vin jaune*'s uniquely oxidized, nutty, yeasty, honeyed, yet almost sour, viscosity. Tissot's 2004 Savagnin is the most stunning we've had. When you hit this Savagnin with Comté, there's an explosion: Nuts, caramel, cream, truffle, yeast, pepper, it keeps going and shifting, until you can't keep up with it; you just have to lie back and breathe.

Cascina degli Ulivi, Filagnotti
& Robiola di Capra Incavolata

I think of Gavi as a very green white wine. The "Fil- agnotti," from Cascina degli Ulivi, conjures the lush splendor of summer afternoons on a terrace, with strong cypress tress all around. In color, it actually holds more sunshine than green hues, as it saturates the glass with spun gold. Tasting of almonds and lemongrass, clay and

unripened plums, its lushness swells beside the clean Robiola di Capra Incavolata from La Casera di Eros. Wrapped
in a cabbage leaf, the cheese's clean milk absorbs garden
notes from the cabbage, even a faint bitterness, which ties
well to the silky greens in the Gavi. When the wine hits
the cheese, its bright sunshine tucks into a perfect cloud
of cream, refreshing you and giving you the chance to
blink at the beauty around you.

ROSÉ

In Paris, Eric and I chortled at the otherwise chic *parisiens*,
moto helmets and Marlboros in abundance, drinking
carafes of rosé at all the hip spots. "How can they think
rosé is cool?" we marveled, associating it more with wine
coolers and cocktails balancing plastic monkeys on a
sugared rim. It turns out that rosé, done well, is quite
cool. Our favorite rosés mix vegetal notes with fruit
and moderate rosé's occasional tang with mineral creaminess.

López de Heredia, Viña Tondonia Rosé (1998) & Robiola di Capra in foglie di Castagno

The color alone would make you wish to drink this rosé
Rioja. It glows with the fiery salmon of sunsets and cop-
pery autumn leaves. The visual mix of midsummer and
autumn plays out in the mouth as well as the glass: Succulent cherry and apricot flavors weigh against a rippling
base of roasted chestnuts. When you pair this cheese with

the Italian Robiola Castagno, a robiola wrapped in chestnut leaves, the musky resonances in both mingle together,
but do not shadow the bright, spreading vista that the
wine and cheese create. This rosé also tastes outstanding
with a perfumey meat like Prosciutto di Parma. Whatever
you eat alongside this wine will glow with the rosé's bor-
rowed light.

Domaine de la Vieille Julienne, Vin de Pays de la Principauté d'Orange (2007) & Candela delle Langhe

I get a thrill from any wines made in Orange, simply
because that principauté is the namesake of Guillaume
d'Orange, medieval knight and hero of French epic poems
(thoughts of chivalry make rosé more delicious). This
domaine is famed for making a stellar Châteauneuf-du-
Pape, but this delicate, nuanced rosé is delight enough
for me. It tastes like fragrances that would emanate from
the splendid Garden of Pleasure depicted in the medieval bestselling verse romance *Le Roman de la Rose*. The wine
savors of tarragon and mint. Sip it, picture the Unicorn
Tapestries, and all those tiny *mille fleurs* will spring to life
in your mouth. A goat cheese decked in flowers, like the
beeswax-covered Candela delle Langhe, will add to those
transports' fragrance. All spring and summer long, in fact,
most goat cheeses will taste of flowers, since the goats love
to eat them. So, choose any young goat cheese, and it will
bloom alongside this evocative wine.

<u>RED</u>

Eric and I enjoy reds best when they have something of the farm about them—soil and herb and even a healthy hit of animal. This profile need not always yield a tongue staining, tannic punch of a wine. Earthy wines can be quite pale in color, herbaceous wines can also be bright and light with ripe cherries, and the animal bit, well, it's just that hint of musk and game that makes you want to eat a steak with it. Trousseau and Poulsard (or Ploussard) from the Jura are aromatic expressions of this flavor range.

Institut Agricole Régional, Petit Rouge & Rosso di Lago

This wine is an argument against the generic Merlots and Cabernet Sauvignons that populate most wine shops. The Institut Agricole Régional, who produces it in Italy's Valle d'Aosta, counts among its missions the preservation and cultivation of unique varietals native to that region. Petit Rouge is one. This wine makes its own case: Where else can you find this fragrance, so floral and herbaceous, a corsage in your glass; where can you find this color, clear garnets; where else this texture, taffeta unrolled on your tongue? I've made it sound effete, but the label sports a large-limbed farmhand in bright colors, and this image works, too, for the wine stakes out the corners of your mouth with earth and dirt. I feel this wine could do anything, be anything, work with any cheese. Rosso di Lago, a creamy cow's milk, appeals visually for its gorgeous umber rind; the light mushroom notes in the *pâte* also offer a perfect palate to foreground the wine's splendor.

G. Descombes, Régnié (2006)
& Vacherin Fribourgeois

I'd never ventured into Beaujolais because I'd noted the scoffs with which those in the know around me greeted the *nouveau* each November. Following their lead, without their experience, I started scoffing anytime someone recommended a Beaujolais. How happy that someone more in the know (thanks, Gemma!) took me down a few notches, by insisting I try this wine. Descombes' 2006 Régnié tastes like the kind of person you'd want to hang out with: self-assured, but not overbearing; complex, but easy to talk with; witty, but with hidden depths. Spice, fruit, tannin, finish, violets, are all in perfect balance. Oh, you well-rounded, amiable Gamay, Beaufort Alpage loves you, Le Drean loves you, Vacherin Fribourgeois loves you. You're the girl next door the cheeses overlooked, but were always meant to fall for. Tasting once, we do.

Cheese Resources

This book has hoped to convince you that cheese, as much as wine, regional cuisines, or the wonders Alice finds through the looking glass, rewards your adventures into it. And Chuck, through a process of choosing that, I can assure you, makes appointments to the Supreme Court look slapdash, has suggested a few choice pairings that might inspire you to try a new taste or return to an old favorite.

This appendix follows her lead in offering information of a practical sort: a list of cheese shops that will ship you many of the cheeses and other goodies that we've mentioned—at least the legal ones—as well as some cheese organizations, festivals, makers, and enthusiasts that will reward your attention. Like Chuck, I have winnowed these selections from the overwhelming possibilities out there, as places to start and with the hope that they will spark your own further adventures into cheese.

GETTING GREAT CHEESE, WHEREVER YOU ARE

Artisanal Premium Cheese: www.artisanalcheese.com

An online cheese extravaganza with cheese tips, cheese

recipes, cheese accessories, a cheese of the month club, as well as scores of cheese from around the world, Artisanal Premium Cheese grew out of Picholine, a two-star Michelin restaurant in New York. It has as its guiding light Max McCalman, America's first restaurant-based *Maître Fromager* and a *Garde et Jure* in France's *Guilde des Fromagers*. At Artisanal, you can order Max's Plate: "3 Cheeses I Love Right Now."

Formaggio Kitchen: www.formaggiokitchen.com

A mom-and-pop (and son-and-daughter) shop for Cantabridgians, Formaggio Kitchen gathers cheese and other singular foods from around the world. The store's owner, Ihsan Gurdal, has been inducted into the *Guilde des Fromagers* and has received the title of *Chevalier* from the *Ordre du Mérite Agricole* for introducing the hand-crafted foods of French artisans to Americans. Formaggio built the first cheese cave in America and treats its cheese with the care that Tiffany does its diamonds. Glorious.

Murray's Cheese: www.murrayscheese.com

The cheese shop started by "a Jewish Spanish civil war veteran and communist who opened a wholesale butter and egg shop a few doors up Cornelia Street in 1940" not only has live mongers on Bleecker Street in Greenwich Village, but also a virtual monger to help you find the perfect cheese. Here's the first question you'll face:

If you were a cheese, would you be:

A. Mozzarella—I can be a little fresh

B. Manchego—Firm and stable, but a little nutty

C. Époisses—My bark is worse than my bite

D. What are Manchego and Époisses?

Murray's has a huge selection of cheeses (including Manchego and Époisses) along with specialty foods and a cheesy sense of humor.

Whole Foods Market: www.wholefoodsmarket.com

Multiplying like the giggles in America, Canada, and the United Kingdom, Whole Foods Markets still support small-scale cheesemakers such as Michael Lee and Peter Dixon. Filled by Global Cheese Buyer Cathy Strange, who is also the Chair of the Cheese of Choice Coalition for the American Cheese Society and a lover of Tallegio, the cheese counters at Whole Foods percolate with raw-milk surprises from the Old World and the New.

CHEESE ENTHUSIASTS

Caseophile: www.fromagium.typepad.com/caseophile

Where should you buy your cheese in Perpignan? In Grenoble? In Châtellerault? What's the skinny on the massive *Salon de l'Agriculture* in Paris or The Cambremer Normandy Festival, and just who's competing this year for the International Caseus Award in Lyon? Marie de Metz Noblat, who has almost two decades of experience as a marketer for French and Swiss cheeses gives English readers a lively look into the French cheese scene.

Cheese by Hand: www.cheesebyhand.com

A cheese-inspired road trip, Cheese by Hand crisscrosses the country to learn about the lives and work of artisanal cheese-makers. The site's creators, Michael Claypool and Sasha Davies, are corporate refugees who decided to get hitched and follow their love of food. They couldn't be more likeable, and the cheery interviews they do showcase the voices of the cheesemakers themselves, talking about their craft, their creations, and the state of farmstead cheese in America.

Cheese Underground:
www.cheeseunderground.blogspot.com

Jeanne Carpenter calls Wisconsin "the Dairy Artisan Mecca of the World" and she's a wonderful guide for would-be pilgrims. Through fun posts and video clips, she introduces you to farmstead cheesemakers in the Amish country of Western Wisconsin, the work of cheese sculptor Sarah Kaufmann, and organizations such as Wisconsin Cheese Originals and the Cheese & Burger Society. Under Jeanne's enthusiastic gaze, not a curd goes unnoticed. She gives "cheese-starved readers everywhere the inside scoop about the state's oldest industry."

The Saxelby Almanac: www.saxelbycheese.blogspot.com

Manhattan's hip monger Anne Saxelby runs a tiny shop in a tiny corner of the Essex Market, where she sells American artisanal cheeses from a tiny case. For all this tininess, Anne's love of cheese couldn't be bigger. She takes asphalt-bound New Yorkers into the countryside to meet farmers and cheesemakers on her "Day A-Whey" trips and hosts a cheese talk-show called "Cutting the Curd," which you can reach through her excellent blog.

THUMBING THROUGH THE CHEESE MAGS

You can't miss the slew of food magazines that fill the shelves of book and grocery stores, but here are a few cheese friendly titles that take a little more looking to find.

> *Alimentum: The Literature of Food:*
>> www.alimentumjournal.com
>
> *The Art of Eating:* www.artofeating.com
>
> *Cheese Enthusiast: The Best of Cheese and Dairy:*
>> www.cheeseenthusiast.net
>
> *Culture: The Word on Cheese:* www.culturecheesemag.com
>
> *Dairy Goat Journal:* www.dairygoatjournal.com
>
> *Gastronomica:* www.gastronomica.org

WHERE'S THE CHEESE CROWD?

New chances to find cheese, cheesemakers, and fellow cheese lovers are springing up everywhere. Here are a few clubs, organizations, and festivals that celebrate cheese, either by promoting it or eating it.

American Cheese Society Annual Conference and
    Competition: www.cheesesociety.org
Boston's Bueno Queso Social Club: www.buenoqueso.org
California's Artisan Cheese Festival:
    www.artisancheesefestival.com
The Cheese School of San Francisco:
    www.cheeseschoolsf.com
Great British Cheese Festival: www.thecheeseweb.com
Great Wisconsin Cheese Festival: www.littlechutewi.org
Hudson Valley Cheese Festival:
    www.hudsonvalleycheesefestival.com
Oregon Cheese Festival: www.oregoncheeseguild.org
Seattle Cheese Festival: www.seattlecheesefestival.com
Slow Food International: www.slowfood.com
Vermont Cheesemakers Festival: www.vtcheesefest.com
Vermont Institute for Artisan Cheese:
    www.nutrition.uvm.edu/viac

Cheesemakers

There are so many artisanal and farmstead cheesemakers whose cheese deserves to find its way to your plate, and since I can't mention them all here, I've included the names of guilds and societies to which many belong and through which you can find them. I've also included some of the cheesemakers whose cheeses appear in this book.

American Cheese Society: www.cheesesociety.org

Ardrahan Farmhouse Cheese: www.ardrahancheese.ie

California Artisan Cheese Guild: www.cacheeseguild.org

Carlisle Farmstead Cheese:
    www.carlislefarmsteadcheese.com

Comité Interprofessionnel du Gruyère de Comté:
    www.comte.com

Consider Bardwell Farm: www.considerbardwellfarm.com

Cypress Grove Chevre: www.cypressgrovechevre.com

Gastronomia Beltrami: www.gastronomiabeltrami.com

Maine Cheese Guild: www.mainecheeseguild.org

New York State Farmstead and Artisan Cheese Makers
    Guild: www.nyfarmcheese.org

Parmigiano-Reggiano Cheese Consortium:
    www.international.parmigiano-reggiano.it

Peter Dixon: www.dairyfoodsconsulting.com

Ontario Cheese Society: www.ontariocheese.org

Oregon Cheese Guild: www.oregoncheeseguild.org

Raw Milk Cheesemakers' Association:
    www.rawmilkcheese.org

Sally Jackson Cheese: www.sallyjacksoncheeses.com

Southern Cheesemakers Guild: www.southerncheese.com

Stilton Cheesemakers' Association: www.stiltoncheese.com

Twig Farm: www.twigfarm.com

The Vermont Cheese Council: www.vtcheese.com

West Country Farmhouse Cheese Makers:
    www.farmhousecheesemakers.com

Widmer's Cheese Cellars: www.widmerscheese.com

Wisconsin Dairy Artisan Network:
    www.wisconsindairyartisan.org

Acknowledgments

This book exists in large part because of the generosity of others. I am happy to thank Robert Aguilera, Ben Day, Lily Kim, Dan Thompkins, Derek Whitaker, and the other members of the Bueno Queso Social Club; Peter Dixon and the cheesemakers at Consider Bardwell Farm; Marie Jo and Maurice Etiévant of Ferme des Nouvelles; Vittorio and Christiana Beltrami of Gastronomia Beltrami; Michael Lee and Emily Sunderman of Twig Farm; Laetitia Robbe and the staff at Fromagerie Marcel Petite; Ishan Gurdal, Kurt Gurdal, Ayse Gurdal, Gemma Iannoni, and the wonderful mongers at Formaggio Kitchen. My thanks go also to Melissa Flashman, Mary LeMay, Daniel Pollack-Pelzner, Ruth Polleys, Amber Qureshi, Damion Searls, and David Seaton for their support, insight, friendship, and help. Material in the book has appeared in *Alimentum*, *Dark Sky Magazine*, and *Gastronomica*, and I thank their editors, Paulette Licitra, Kevin Murphy, and Darra Goldstein. In writing this book, I've drawn on the work of many excellent food writers and cheese professionals, among them Pierre Androuët, Edward Behr, Michael Claypool, Sasha Davies, Steven Jenkins, Max McCalman, Heather Paxton, and Amy Trubek, and I am indebted to them. My greatest debt belongs to Chuck, *pâte* to my rind.

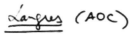

Langres (AOC)

convex top. caves into pour in wine (champagne).
bright orange tone.
bumpy texture very pronounced on top— missing on sides.
Smooth sides.
total size: 3 in diameter.
2.5 in tall.

firm rind.
light molding in white + a few blue patches.

Smells like— smoked Gouda.

Terrible drawing!
WORST yet!!

Chuck's sketch of the cheese that started it all.

About the Author

Eric LeMay has received an MFA from Columbia and a PhD in English Renaissance literature from Northwestern University. He has won multiple awards for his teaching at Harvard, Northwestern, and the University of Chicago. He has worked as an editor at *TriQuarterly* and is now the Web editor of *Alimentum: The Literature of Food*. His previous work has appeared in *Gastronomica*, *The Nation*, *The Paris Review*, and *The Harvard Review*; it has been noted in the *Best American Essays* series, featured on *Poetry Daily*, and selected for *Best Food Writing*. He has published one book of poems. He and his cotaster Chuck were longtime members of Boston's Bueno Queso Social Club, a cheery mishmash of cheesemongers, wine importers, beer sellers, chefs, and gastronomes, before getting married and moving to New York City, where they now haunt the city's cheese shops. Visit his Web site at www.ericlemay.org.